Alexander W Winter

Winter's Handy Book of Reference

for packers, butchers, abattoirs, meat markets and stockmen; meat markets and stockmen

Alexander W Winter

Winter's Handy Book of Reference
for packers, butchers, abattoirs, meat markets and stockmen; meat markets and stockmen

ISBN/EAN: 9783337254407

Printed in Europe, USA, Canada, Australia, Japan

Cover: Foto ©Lupo / pixelio.de

More available books at **www.hansebooks.com**

WINTER'S
Handy Book of Reference

FOR PACKERS, BUTCHERS, ABATTOIRS, MEAT MARKETS AND STOCKMEN

CONTAINING FORMULAS FOR MAKING ALL GRADES OF LARD AND PROCESSES FOR BLEACHING, DEODORIZING AND CLARIFYING LARD, TALLOW, GREASES AND OILS; ALSO FOR MANUFACTURING FERTILIZERS, TAKING CARE OF BONES, BLOOD AND OFFAL

GIVING FULL PARTICULARS AS TO THE
MANUFACTURE OF BUTTERINE, COTTOLENE, VEGETABLE COTTO-SUET, ETC., ETC.

BY ALEXANDER W. WINTER

Author of "The Packers' and Refiners' Encyclopedia"

CHICAGO
LAIRD & LEE, PUBLISHERS

Read! Read! Read!

Here are a few recipes that are to be found in Winter's Handy Book of Reference that will alone pay you one hundred times in one short season the outlay for the book.

First: Every butcher knows that he has fats and scraps, commonly termed shop fat. This he sells and gets very little for and very often gives it away in order to get rid of it, especially in summer. He also knows what an annoyance it is in summer and how it fills his shop with blow flies, and how it smells and what a terrible nuisance it is. Now, do you know that this very scrap will more than pay your rent, your help and the care and feed of your horse, if you take proper care of it, not speaking of the cleanness of your shop? How to do it is what troubles you, but you know others do it. *Why don't you?* Buy one of these books for five dollars and see how easy and simple it is.

Next: During hot weather the trouble comes. Your lard is too soft, it won't stand up; can't sell it; have to stop making it. Do you know that the very stuff you throw amongst your shop fat and the very stuff that you are giving away is the very thing that is utilized in mixing with your lard to make it stiff, firm and in such shape that the texture is like butter instead of like mush? Think of it—see what a saving. Others are saving this and making big money out of it. You can do the same. Why don't you? Read Winter's five dollar book. Post yourself and be ready when the time comes to do what all wide-awake butchers are doing.

Then again: You all know you have everlasting trouble with your lard about the color. Once it is just right, next day it is yellow, next time it is brown, next time it is dark, etc. You keep on guessing, and trying and experimenting and still you can't find out what the trouble is. If a man should come along just about that time and say: "I can show you a process that will overcome all this trouble," you would willingly pay him fifty dollars for the receipt. Here in Winter's handy book, etc., you find this receipt and many others for five dollars. Secure one at once, as only enough will be printed to fill advance orders.

Hundreds of wide-awake packers, butchers, fertilizers, soap and candle manufacturers have already sent in their subscriptions. You can't compete with these people if you don't keep up with the times. Secure a book at once and learn what others are doing.

To Pork Packers, Lard Refiners, Butchers, Beef Slaughterers, Meat Markets, Abattoirs, Etc.

After having published the Packers' and Refiners' Encyclopedia, I concluded to publish no more books, but to give my whole time and attention to my business, viz.: fitting up refineries, furnishing formulas and processes to those who desired them, and leave the publishing of books to others who might be more able than I to write them. But after furnishing my book to hundreds of subscribers, many letters came to me daily for more information and inquiries for a book that would not cost so much money. This Encyclopedia was sold for fifteen dollars per copy, and I find thousands who wanted the book were unable to pay that price, and wrote to inquire if I could furnish them with a book for less money. Having had so many inquiries of this sort, I consulted with the publishers and find I can put a book on the market for five dollars per copy, providing that I get subscribers enough to it. I therefore send you a contract and ask you to sign it for a copy of this book, should you desire one. I will say here, the same as I did in publishing the Encyclopedia, that only enough books will be published to fill the orders on hand. After the Encyclopedia was published hundreds of letters came, asking for copies, but as I made contracts for only enough to fill subscribers' orders it was impossible to publish more. This edition will positively be the last one published by me, and as it will contain formulas for making all grades of lard, for bleaching, deodorizing and clarifying lards, tallow, greases and oils; also for the manufacture of fertilizer, taking care of the bones, blood and offal, give full particulars as to the manufacture of butterine, cottolene, vegetable cotto-suet, etc., it will certainly be a cheap book and one that every butcher, meat market, refinery, packing house, etc., should have.

In conclusion I would say, that during the past years I have been Superintendent and Manager of the Mission Soap and Candle Works, San Francisco, Cal.; Bay Soap and Candle Works, San Francisco; Superintendent and Manager for the Commercial Manufacturing Co., manufacturing oleomargarine, etc., a concern incorporated with a capital of $10,000,000; Superintendent of the Electric Candle Co., of New York; Refiner for the Armour Packing Co., Kansas City. I have also fitted up the refineries of Swift & Co., Chicago; T. E. Wells Co., Chicago; International Packing and Provision Co., Chicago; Minneapolis Provision Co., Minneapolis; Parker, Webb & Co., Detroit, Mich.; Ed. Haakinson & Co., Sioux City, Ia.; Jacob Packing Co., Cincinnati; Masterman & Co., Montreal; Thomas Lowry & Son, Hamilton, Ont.; Superintended Dominion Manufacturing and Exporting Co., Montreal; and others.

LIST OF CONTENTS.

Killing department.
Cutting room.
Rendering room.

LARD DEPARTMENT OF THE PACKING HOUSE.

Processes for manufacturing lards:
    Pure kettle lard.
    Prime steam.
    Choice family.
    Cottolene.
    Lard compound.
    Silver leaf.
    Imitation steam lard.
    Cuba lard.
    Watered lard.
Processes for refining lard.
Processes for bleaching lard, oils, tallow and greases.
Processes for deodorizing the same.
Processes for clarifying the same.
How to pack lard: Size of packages used.

How to put crimp on lard to imitate pure kettle leaf.

How to properly fit up the filter so it can be readily cleaned without the loss of a particle of lard.

Special table for figuring hardness for different climates, so that in shipping to warm or cold countries the lard will be of proper texture.

Best formulas for maknig lards that will not crumble.

Best modes of rendering tallow with water and steam.

How to harden tallow.

How to bleach tallow by exposure and by chemicals.

Selection and preparation of fats for oleomargarine.

How to manufacture oleomargarine, oleo oil, oleo butter and butterine.

How to prepare the leaf for making neutral.

How to make wet and dry neutral.

Latest and most improved modes of caring for bones, blood and offal.

How to make fatty acid tests.

How to adulterate oils.

Solution and glasses required for making free acid tests.

PORK HOUSE DEPARTMENT.

Irish cut sides: How packed and made.

Extra prime pork: How packed, cut and made.

Barrel backs: How packed and how much salt required.

Cured meats: What is required by the Board of Trade throughout the United States.

Breakfast bacon: How cut, what weight, etc.

Sweet or plain pickled bellies: How made, cut and trmimed.

Also in cutting different meats: How they should be classified and cut.

How to cure and pack:
    Beef hams.
    Beef tongues.
    Plate beef.
    American short cut pork tongues.
    Extra India mess beef.
    Extra family beef.
    Extra packet beef.
    Extra mess beef.

It will also fully explain the requirements of the Board of Trade for the classification of lard:
    Prime steam lard.
    Refined lard.
    Choice lard.

Neutral lard.

Pure leaf lard.

Also how to cut mess pork: What each barrel should contain.

Prime mess pork: How to make, how much salt, how much brine, what strength, how much saltpeter, and how the barrels are to be coopered.

Rib bellies: How to be cut, packed and how to classify; how the boxes shall be made and what each box shall weigh.

How to cut and pack clear bellies.

How to pack short clear middles.

Extra short clears: How packed.

Cumberland cut: How packed and cut.

    Short clear middles.

    Short cut mess pork.

    Long rib middles.

    Birmingham sides.

    South Staffordshire sides.

    Yorkshire sides.

    Long clears.

    Whiteshire sides.

    Extra long clears.

    Short clear backs.

    Long fat backs.

    Short fat backs.

Short rib sides (Chicago Board of Trade sellers' option).
New York shoulders.
Boston shoulders.
American short cut hams.
Straffordshire hams.
Manchester hams.
Three rib square shoulders.
Rolled hams, boneless.
Rolled shoulders, boneless.
California hams.
Short cut clear pork.
Export short ribs.
The best fuller's earth.

And many other valuable receipts, processes and practical suggestions most useful to the trade.

INTRODUCTION

The great importance of the swine breeding industry is evident, as we consider that there are about 47,000,000 hogs raised during the summer season in the United States. The number annually slaughtered is about 28,000,000, and the consumption is estimated at seventy pounds to each inhabitant, or 4,000,000,000 lbs. The annual exportation for twenty-five years, including hogs with pork product, has been 530,000,000 pounds. The average weight of swine dressed was 175 lbs.

The large corn supply and moderate prices account for the good condition of the hogs. There has been a marked exemption from wide-spread disease during the year, though in some countries South and West cholera has prevailed, in consequence of severe weather, scarcity of food, and the feeding of unmatured corn. That the extent of this industry is largely commensurate with the corn product, and that its geographical distribution is defined by our corn territory is a statement which, in itself, is a demonstration; it is estimated that the value of hogs annually slaughtered in the United States is $393,570,-000. The following is a list of States in order of the production of swine: Iowa, Illinois, Ohio, Missouri, Indiana, Kansas, Nebraska, Wisconsin, Tennessee and Kentucky.

The live hogs which furnish the basis of our large packing houses are largely purchased in the West, and shipped and transported direct to the packing-houses in the latest and most improved stock cars. Here they are unloaded, placed in their respective pens and sold. The slaughtering of hogs, rendering, curing, packing, jobbing, and exporting the product of same, together with packing of beef and general distribution of fresh and cured meats to all markets of the world constitute the business of our largest packers. The packing-houses in Chicago for the various manufacturing of products handled by them occupy many acres of land, all covered with substantial brick buildings, equipped with the latest and most improved machinery, packers always keeping one great secret in mind, and that is to handle their products in an economical and systematic manner. The motto of the large and successful packers has always been, to handle the large quantities with as little labor as possible.

The main building and connections of some of our large packers are over 800 feet long, and over 175 feet wide, and from three to eight stories high. The offices are large, spacious, airy and very convenient, and accommodate a large working force which consists of: The superintendent, manager, paymaster, bookkeepers, entry and receiving clerks, the auditors, and shipping and time clerks.

Other buildings consist of engine-rooms, boiler rooms, electrical and ice-machine plants, blacksmith shops, wheelwright and general repair shops car shops, stables, wholesale and retail markets, steam-cooperage plants, cold-storage warehouses, some having a capacity of one hundred thousand barrels, and besides the cold storage houses there are acres of floor surface under refrigeration in other buildings, the entire plant having a capacity of handling from seven to ten thousand hogs per day.

These buildings are located at the Union Stock Yards, about three and one-half miles from the court house, in close proximity to all rail transportation, and all railroads enter the yards by which live animals and other supplies are received, and a large amount of the manufactured product is delivered to the wharves of the Atlantic Steamship lines for export and coast-wise trade, and car-loads are delivered to interior points in this country direct from the packing-houses.

Track facilities are there to accommodate hundreds of cars at a time. In fitting up a packing-house it should be the aim of the packer to endeavor to unload his hogs direct from the car into the run or air-shaft, which will land them in the killing room on the top floor. This air-shaft should be well lighted and ventilated.

Here they are slaughtered and then passed to the dressing-room, where the hair and bristles are removed by machinery, after which the hog passes to the scraping and shaving bench, from which he is taken on a railway to the open air cooling-room, which should have a capacity of hanging a thousand hogs, more or less. Here they should remain for a limited time, when the animal heat is out of them; then they are put into the cooler, which is either cooled by refrigeration or ice. From here the hog is passed into the cutting-room, where he is manufactured into all cuts adaptable for the different markets of the world. There should be a large separate floor for the curing of various cuts of meat which are cured in dry salt for the English and foreign markets, for which this meat is made; then again, another floor should be used for curing pickled meats for domestic and other markets. The entire building in which the hog is cut and cured should be of a uniform temperature at all seasons of the year and must be either refrigerated by ice or machinery.

When the meats are cured and ready for shipment on orders, they should be conveyed to another department used only for storage supplies.

None but thoroughly competent men should be employed and only such as have had experience. The various brands of meat should be uniformly and regularly cut. Many of the most popular and well-known cuts and descriptions will now be given on the following pages.

STANDARD BOARD OF TRADE RULES
CURED MEATS

Where sales of meat are made with other specifications, it shall be considered that meats taken are merchantable meats fully cured, and if no special brand is sold with them the meat so sold shall be up to the average of the packer's brand who offers or sells the same. While the rules explained herein with the different cuts of meat may be varied at times somewhat, they are nearly the standard rules governing most of the Boards of Trade throughout the United States, each packer, in case of disputes, being subjected to his local Board of Trade rules in the market where the goods are packed.

In cutting of all the different cuts of meat, pieces shall be classified light, medium, and heavy, and packed separately, as nearly as practicable, in boxes made to fit the meat, due attention being paid to the average and uniformity to said average as packed. The nearer the meat is sized to the average sold, the better the reputation of the brand, if well cut and cured and due attention paid to curing for markets intended for, whether mild with fine color, heavily salted for warm climates, or to keep for a long time.

CLASSIFICATION OF LARD

PRIME STEAM LARD

Prime steam lard shall be solely the natural product of the trimmings and other fat parts of hogs, rendered in tanks by the direct application of steam and without subsequent change in grain or character by the use of agitators or other machinery, except as such changes may unavoidably come from transportation. It shall have proper color, flavor, and soundness for keeping, and no material which has been salted shall be included. The name and location of the renderer and the grade of the lard shall be plainly branded on each package at the time of packing.

REFINED LARD

May be offered and sold on the brand; when sold in tierces, the renderer's name and place of production shall be distinctly marked on each tierce, at the time of packing, with marking iron and stencil.

CHOICE LARD

Shall be equal in quality to lard made from leaf and trimmings, and shall be properly rendered as to color, flavor, and soundness for keeping. All tierces and tubs must have gross weights and tares marked on them.

NEUTRAL LARD

Made entirely from raw leaf, being first hashed and then rendered at a low temperature, then agitated for a short time, cooled and grained to suit the market. It is principally used in the manufacture of butterine, makes a very fine product and if properly rendered should be perfectly neutral in taste and smell.

PURE LEAF LARD

Is rendered in jacket kettles; it is made from leaf lard without any other ingredients, and packed in tierces, tins, pails, and in such packages as the trade may require. Of course at present very little leaf is put into lard, for the simple reason that the leaf when rendered for neutral brings a much better price than when put it into lard.

CLASSIFICATION OF BEEF

BEEF HAMS

Usually cut in three pieces, from the leg of medium-width beeves, packed fresh in barrels, two hundred and twenty pounds of green meat to the barrel, cured in sweet pickle, according to the formula of the packer similar to hams.

After being cured, this beef is also dried by means of a dry-house, to make the dried beef of commerce; put up to suit any market.

BEEF TONGUES

Cured in sweet pickle accordingto the standard of the packer, root of tongue largely taken off forty-five to fifty tongues to the barrel.

EXTRA PACKET BEEF

Is a light grade of plate beef, packed uniform with proportionate pieces from the rattle; packed in barrels of two hundred pounds, and in tierces of three hundred and four pounds.

EXTRA MESS BEEF

Made from the fore quarter of light-weight cattle, with due proportion of rib, rump, flank, and sirloin, although this formula varies somewhat from different packers who brand their name on Extra Mess Beef.

EXTRA INDIA MESS BEEF

Cut from the rattle from heavy fore quarters of fat beeves in nearly uniform eight-pound pieces, due proportion brisket, standing rib, and navel being packed to each tierce of three hundred and four pounds. This is a high grade heavy, fat beef, sold largely for export.

EXTRA FAMILY BEEF

Is from heavy, fat cattle, cut from the rattle, and a heavier grade than plate beef, having a fair proportion of standing rib, brisket, and navel cuts distributed proportionately throughout the barrel.

Packed two hundred pounds used largely for export and is also packed in half barrels and tierces when required.

PLATE BEEF

Composed of uniform plates, ribs, navels, some brisket and a lighter grade of beef than family.

AMERICAN SHORT CUT PORK TONGUES

Roots all cut off, cured in sweet pickle. For the American market two hundred pounds to the barrel English market, two hundred and twenty-four pounds to the barrel. Cured in mild pickle according to the formula of the packer, and suited to the needs of any market.

RECIPE NO. 1

PURE KETTLE LARD

In order to make a Pure Kettle Lard, the leaf lard of the hog is taken and hashed, and from the hasher it is run into a jacket kettle, which should be provided with an agitator.

It is then heated and cooked for about six hours, at a temperature of 240 degrees Fahrenheit, the agitator continually turning the stock.

It is then allowed to settle and is run off into packages.

While cooking this stock, use say 20 lbs. of salt to a batch of 5,000 lbs. of leaf lard, for settling purposes.

The remaining stock, after the pure kettle lard has run off, is either put into the tanks for prime steam, or it can be pressed and the cracklings sold for feeding hogs; but it is preferable and best to take the whole mess and put it into the prime steam tank.

RECIPE NO. 2

KETTLE RENDERED LARD

A fine kettle rendered lard is made by using

    20 lbs. Leaf Lard
    12 lbs. Lard-stearine
    68 lbs. Back Fat
    ―――
    100 lbs. Kettle Rendered Lard.

Cook four hours at a temperature of 260 degrees Fahrenheit. Let the stock cook two hours, then add ten pounds of salt. Then cook for two hours longer, add ten pounds more salt and allow all to settle for half an hour. Then draw into a settling tank and allow it to settle for one hour. It is then ready for drawing into packages. The agitator in the kettle should run at the rate of about thirty revolutions a minute. The lard should be drawn for tins at about 200 degrees Fahrenheit and for tierces at from 100 to 110 degrees Fahrenheit.

RECIPE NO. 3

PRIME STEAM LARD

In order to make a choice Prime Steam Lard, the stock should be cooked immediately. Laying it over and holding it until you have enough for a full tank, always makes the lard of an inferior standard. But if the tanks are in readiness immediately after the killing and the stock is placed in them at once, it will make a fine white lard.

Prime steam lard should be cooked for about eight hours, under a steam pressure of 60 lbs.

I would recommend cooking it, for about two hours at the start, with plenty of water. Then allow it to settle and draw the water off; then put in fresh water and finish cooking.

Of course, in cooking this stock, it is important to always have the pet cocks on the top of the tank blowing off, so as to allow the gases to escape.

Have your tanks so arranged that the water will go in from the bottom and not from the top, as I have seen it often done The water-pipes being so arranged that it flows in from the bottom, it will allow you to raise the lard up to the cocks and draw it off to the last particle. The water must be let in slowly.

After all of the lard is off, the drop-door is let fall and the whole mess dropped into a tank, where it is carefully skimmed.

Then the water is run off, and the remaining stock pressed in a tankage press.

The tankage is then taken to the Anderson drier and fertilizer made out of it.

RECIPE NO. 4

CHOICE FAMILY LARD

This is a grade of lard that is generally made out of

- 40 lbs. Lard
- 20 lbs. Tallow
- 20 lbs. Cotton Oil
- 20 lbs Off Lard

100 lbs. Choice Family Lard.

RECIPE NO. 5

COTTOLINE

Cottolene is made out of cotton oil and oleo-stearine in the following proportions:

    60 lbs. Cotton Oil
    40 lbs. Oleo-stearine
    ―――――――――
    100 lbs Cottoline.

To make a good cottolene, this stock is never bleached or refined, but should have a nice grain and be of a yellow color.

It should not be heated too highly. I have always found that it was best flavored when heated at a temperature of not more than 180 degrees Fahrenheit.

It is used by bakers and is in growing demand.

After it is heated to 180 degrees Fahrenheit, put the blower on.

Blow well until all is dissolved and thoroughly mixed.

No fuller's earth or other refining stock must be used.

After it is all well mixed and properly heated,

start the pump, and pump the cottolene through a filter.

Then pass it over the roller into the agitator and finally draw into tierces or other packages as desired.

RECIPE NO. 6

LARD COMPOUND

Lard Compound is made out of
- 60 lbs. Cotton Oil
- 20 lbs. Deodorized Hog Grease
- 10 lbs. Tallow
- 10 lbs. Oleo-stearine

100 lbs. Lard Compound,

RECIPE NO. 7

SILVER LEAF LARD

This grade of lard may be made out of prime steam lard; the proportions are:

    80 lbs. Prime Steam Lard
    20 lbs. Lard-stearine
    ―――
    100 lbs. Silver Leaf Lard.

During the months of June, July and August, fully 25 to 30 per cent lard-stearine is used. When the cooler weather sets in and all through the winter months, no lard-stearine is used.

This grade of lard, if properly refined, makes a beautiful pure-white lard and sells rapidly.

It is packed in tins of 3, 5, 10, 20 and 50 lbs.; also in all sizes of wooden packages and tierces.

In making this grade of lard, I would suggest that in tanking the prime steam lard for the purpose of manufacturing silver leaf lard one should arrange it so as to use a considerable quantity of back fat in this grade.

RECIPE NO. 8

IMITATION STEAM LARD

Imitation Steam Lard is made out of

    60 lbs. Lard
    40 lbs. Tallow
   —
    100 lbs. Imitation Steam Lard.

The 60 per cent of lard trimmings and the 40 per cent of tallow trimmings, are put into the lard tanks, and with it, if possible, some of the remaining stock from kettle-lard.

It is then cooked and handled the same as the prime steam lard.

I have tanked lard on this formula and cooked it well, so that it had precisely the same flavor as a pure prime steam, and could pass for a steam lard.

RECIPE NO. 9

CUBA LARD

My experience with Cuba lard has been that in shipping to Cuba, a great deal depends on the party to whom the lard is shipped.

Some of the dealers in Cuba want a strictly prime steam lard. This is packed in tins of different sizes.

Then again, some trade wants a lard that is made somewhat like our imitation steam lard.

Then again, some want it with 40 per cent water.

I have found it a difficult trade to satisfy, unless it is in the supply of pure steam lard.

The following are some of the formulas I have used when manufacturing Cuba lard for a large packing house:

 30 lbs. Lard
 10 lbs. White Deodorized Grease
 40 lbs. Tallow
 20 lbs. Cotton Oil
 ———
100 lbs. Cuba Lard.

30 lbs. Lard
10 lbs. White Deodorized Grease
40 lbs. Tallow
20 lbs. Jawbone Stock
───
100 lbs. Cuba Lard.

60 lbs. Tallow
25 lbs. White Deodorized Grease
15 lbs. Cotton Oil
───
100 lbs. Cuba Lard.
To this add 20 per cent Water

75 lbs. Tallow
25 lbs. White Deodorized Grease
───
100 lbs. Cuba Lard.

RECIPE NO. 10

WATERED LARD

In order to make a Watered Lard, you take say one barrel of the best "plasterer's lime;" this you stock with about five or six barrels of water.

Let your man stir the lime well and get it thoroughly dissolved, then allow it to settle and use the liquor; this will be of a clear blue color.

Now to use it you take such percentage as you desire to carry, and when the lard is in the agitator, you let the water run in slowly, allowing the agitator to work steadily for one hour after the water is in, also while the water is running into this lard. Let the agitator continue in motion until all of the lard is drawn off, not drawing off any lard, however, before you have made sure that all the water has been taken up and is thoroughly mixed with the lard.

RECIPE NO. 11

PROCESSES FOR REFINING LARD

Run the lard to be refined into a jacket kettle.

A. REFINING SILVER LEAF LARD

Heat up to 190 degrees Fahrenheit. Start the blower and, when all is melted, put in about 3 per cent fuller's earth and let the blower mix it well.

When the earth is in the lard, and the blower has run, say four or five minutes, start your pump and pump through the filter. The lard should come out as clear as distilled water.

Let the blower work all the time you are pumping, so as not to let the fuller's earth settle.

B. REFINING CHOICE FAMILY LARD

Put your ingredients into the jacket tank and heat to about 215 to 220 degrees Fahrenheit; then add about 7 per cent fuller's earth, and let it be well blown by the blower.

When it is well mixed and agitated, start the pump and run the lard through the filter into the receiver; then over the roller into the agitator, and then pack in such packages as you desire.

C. REFINING LARD COMPOUND

This operation is done by means of the recipe relating to the refining of Choice Family Lard, the only difference being that you may be obliged to use a little more fuller's earth than on the Choice Family Lard.

RECIPE NO. 12

PROCESS FOR BLEACHING LARDS, OILS, TALLOWS AND GREASES

When it is desired to bleach lards, oils, tallows or greases, the products are put into jacket tanks and heated to about 215 degrees Fahrenheit, and fuller's earth is added until the desired color is obtained.

The process for treating these ingredients will be found fully explained in the preceding recipes.

RECIPE NO. 13

PROCESS FOR DEODORIZING LARDS, OILS, TALLOWS AND GREASES

Here is undoubtedly the best deodorizing process, and it is known only to a very few.

For twenty barrels of grease or oil take four pounds of permanganate of potash, with three pounds of bichromate of potash and one pound of sal soda.

Dissolve together in the chemical tank, in five barrels of water, the bichromate of potash and the soda; then put in the permanganate of potash and dissolve that. Then allow this solution to run into the grease.

Turn on the air and mix the chemical solution and the grease or oil; then add sulphuric acid of 66 degrees Beaume, diluted with half water. Add this acid in the proportion of one quart clear acid to each pound of the chemicals.

When the reaction takes place and the grease turns to a green color, turn on steam in addition to the air, and allow the air to continue for five minutes; then shut off the air and bring to a lively boil.

When boiled, shut off steam and allow to settle; it will take ten to twenty minutes. Then draw off the chemical water and spray with a hose thoroughly, using clear water. Allow it to settle and draw off this water. Then make a mixture of one-half pound sal soda in one tierce of water and pour it into the washing tank.

Run the bleached grease into this and boil two hours and then allow the water to settle.

This is for poor grades of stock that you want deodorized.

In treating any quantity of grease or oil it will only be necessary to change the quantity of the chemicals in the same proportion. To deodorize white grease or smothered hog grease from all bad odor, a one-pound mixture is sufficient for each barrel. Use, in that case, the following mixture:

> One-half lb. Permanganate of Potash
> Three-eighths lb. Bichromate of Potash
> One-eighth lb. Sal Soda

Total, One lb. Chemicals.

In using acid, it will be sufficient to use one quart of pure sulphuric acid to each pound of chemicals used as above, diluting the acid one-half with water, always figuring on the addition of pure acid; then dilute.

Just at this point I think a few words regarding the use and manipulation of smothered hogs, or hogs that have died of disease, may be in order. It may not be known to the smaller packers in the smaller towns to what an extent such animals are used in the manufacture of the cheaper grades of lard. In the smaller towns and neighborhoods such animals are generally buried. They can generally be obtained from the farmers for hauling them away. It is a very simple matter to render them in a tank, the whole carcass being thrown in and thoroughly boiled. After boiling, allow it to settle thoroughly. Skim off the lard and treat it as directed in Recipe No. 13, and the result will be a beautifully clear, white and odorless lard. When it is considered that a three hundred pound hog, treated as above shown, will yield about 130 pounds of lard that will sell readily for six cents per pound, it will be evident that this is a branch of the business that is well worth looking into.

The residue of the animal may be used for fertilizer, as directed in Recipes Nos. 31, 32 and 33. Great caution must be exercised in handling such animals. I have seen them lying on the platforms at the Union Stock Yards, Chicago, swollen to twice their natural size and burst open. They should *always* be handled with hooks or with gloves. If handled with naked hands on which there is the slightest scratch or sore, blood poisoning is almost sure to follow and cause most serious trouble. It will be seen from the above that the careful manipulation of such animals by *careful people* will bring good returns to many who have heretofore given no attention to anything of the kind. Fats of any other animals than hogs may be thoroughly deodorized by the use of Recipe No. 13, pressed by a lever press and the oil used for lubricating purposes, and the stearine sold to soap manufacturers or used in *any mixture* or for *any purpose* that the manipulator may desire.

A tank to treat 20 tierces should be 4 ft. in diameter at the bottom, 7 ft. diameter at the top and 10 ft. high. The staves, 2 inches thick, to be all of clear, kiln-dried pine, bottom dished to center one inch; the tank should have 9 hoops, each with clamps of round iron. Estimated cost: $75.00.

A TEST OF THE ABOVE RECIPE

To make a small test of this most valuable

recipe, take a 4-ounce bottle, fill it quarter full with the stock to be tested; add one-third size of bottle of the chemicals mixed in above proportions; add a little sulphuric acid; shake it well until the mixture assumes a light color, then add a little live steam, using a small hose or pipe for the purpose; then boil for thirty seconds. The bottle will not break if it is a regular 4-ounce bottle. After this, allow the matter to settle. This will at once show whether the grease will pay for handling it.

A FEW SPECIAL POINTS CONCERNING RECIPE NO 13

Be sure to use oil of vitriol of 66 degrees Beaume, and mix it in one half water.

In starting to deodorize do not use any steam, as the stock, if steamed out of the tierces, will be heated, and the chemicals will keep it at the proper heat.

The deodorizing tank is to be of wood, with a lead pipe for introducing steam, and a connection at the top, as shown in the drawing, for introducing air at the bottom. Be sure to see that no iron connections are used in this tank; have only regular fittings *for acid use.*

The first step, to start with, is to steam the stock to be used out of the tierces into the deodorizing tank. After it is in the tank, let it settle and draw off the water from the bottom. Put the blower on and allow air to enter; then let the chemicals run in; the stock will then turn a very black color. Then run in the acid and let the reaction take place. Keep the blower going until the stock changes color; it will soon do so, becoming lighter and lighter. This will take about half an hour; then add open steam. Keep boiling, with the blower and open steam on, until the stock comes to a boil; then shut off the blower, but let the open steam continue. Boil the stock for about five or ten minutes; then allow it to settle and draw off the water saturated with chemicals. Fresh water is then added with the hose in a thorough spray. No blowing or boiling is necessary during this operation. Allow the stock to settle; draw off the water and repeat. Then run the stock into the wash tank and boil with open steam. Be sure to have the sal soda, spoken of above, in this tank and boil hard.

Have two small tanks above the deodorizing tanks, the acid tank to hold two barrels and the chemical tank five barrels; the acid tank must be lined with lead. The arrangement of tanks can be seen at a glance by referring to the full-page engraving on the opposite page.

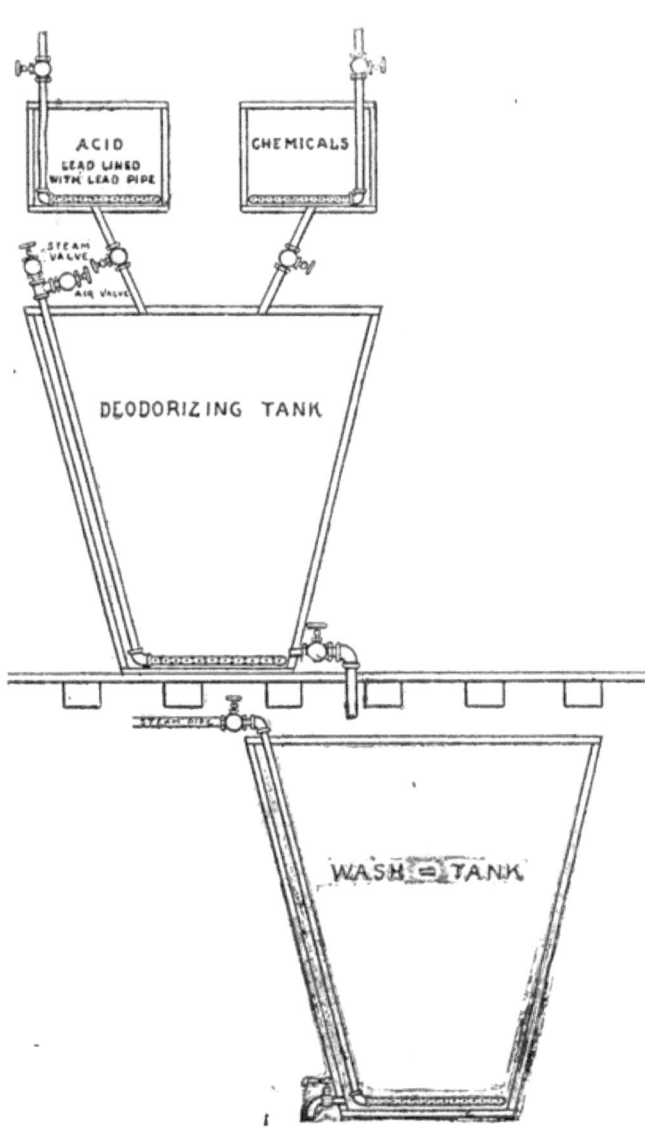

RECIPE NO. 14

PROCESS FOR CLARIFYING LARDS, OILS, TALLOWS AND GREASES

To clarify lards, oils, tallows and grease, the heat in the jacket kettle must reach 230 degrees Fahrenheit; let the blower agitate the stock for two hours at that temperature.

Then pump through the filter and let the stock cool in the receiver; draw off when cooled.

Never draw oil into barrels when it is hot or even simply warm. Let it be well chilled before drawing; otherwise your oil will be cloudy.

SUGGESTIONS AS TO MACHINERY NEEDED FOR THE PROPER WORKING OF THE PRECEDING PROCESSES

The machinery required for an ordinary lard, oil and grease refinery is to be composed of:

I. A Jacket Kettle.
II. One Blower-Pump Engine.
III. One Filter of 36 Plates, 24 Inches in Diameter, with Cocks on Each Plate.

ADVANTAGES GAINED BY THE FILTER PRESS OVER OLD TIME METHODS OF SEPARATING SOLIDS FROM LIQUIDS

1st. Economy of Space. The method adopted of distributing the filtering surface in the filter press secures an enormous filtering area within a comparatively small space.

2d. Saving of Time. What formerly took months to accomplish in the settling tank can now be done in an hour with the filter press.

3d. Quality of Work Done. All solid impurities, no matter what their size or specific gravity may be, are completely removed from the liquid.

4th. Quantity of Work Done. The material to be filtered is forced through the filtered press under high pressure; consequently, large quantities can be filtered in a very short time.

5th. Complete Separation of the Oil from the Cake, as in the case of decolorizing oils, lards and greases with fuller's earth. The earth during filtration is collected in the form of compact cakes containing some of the oil or grease, which can be removed completely by steaming the cake before taking it from the filter press, no handling afterwards being necessary.

DESCRIPTION OF THE FILTER PRESS

Since the introduction of the filter press, all other modes for separating and collecting precipitates from liquids have become obsolete. The filter press consists of a series of round or square plates, made of cast iron, lead, hard wood or other suitable material, having projecting lugs, so that they can be supported in a press frame, in juxtaposition, face to face, and screwed up tightly between the head and follower of the press. The plates are concave on each side, while the projecting, truly-faced rims maintain the plate surfaces at distances corresponding to the depth of two rims. Faced rings can be inserted between the rims of two plates, to increase the distance between their surfaces. The plates, provided with channels communicating with outlets at the bottom, are covered with suitable filtering cloth. Thus the spaces between the cloth-lined plates form chambers, into which the semi-fluid material to be filtered is forced under pressure. A passage, also lined with cloth, is formed through each plate, so that there is communication between all the filtering chambers. A pair of cloths are used to cover each side of a plate, sewed together round a center-hole, corresponding to the opening in the plate. It is obvious that on folding one cloth, passing it through the hole in the plate, and then opening it out, both surfaces of the latter will be covered. The hooks on the plates, to which the filtering cloth is fastened, are movable by means of screw spindles, so that slackness of the filters can be taken up in a radial direction, thus insuring tight joints between the plates. The material for the filters, which must combine strength, durability and closeness of texture, is specially manufactured and called "lamb-skin." When the solution to be filtered is forced into the chambers of the press, the liquid is driven through the cloth, and flows away through the outlets at the bottom of the plates, while the solid matter is arrested in the chambers. Finally, when the solid matter fills every chamber completely, the operation of charging is suspended. This is indicated by the filtrate ceasing to flow from the outlets of the plates at the maximum pressure, say 150 pounds per square inch, for which the press is designed. Now the press is unscrewed, the plates are separated, and, without removing the filters, the chambers are emptied, their contents being in the form of solid cakes with more or less moisture, according to the character of the precipitate and the pressure in charging. The latter is indicated by a pressure-gauge. It does not take more than one minute to unload each chamber.

These machines are also constructed with square plates, and, in some special cases, arranged for using filtering paper instead of cloth as the filtering medium.

To do first-class work economically, it is necessary to be provided with first-class apparatus.

I have used various machines and appliances for filtering oils, greases, lard, etc., but the above described filter press has always given me such thorough satisfaction that I strongly recommend its use to those who adopt any of my various processes requiring filtration. Personally, I have always selected this machine for my various filtering operations.

IV. One Duplex Pump, 4 x 6 x 4.

V. One Iron Receiver, Capacity 10,000 Lbs. This is to be placed directly under the filter, so as to catch the stock that is pumped through the filter.

VI. One Cylinder Roller, 9 Feet Long and 4 Feet in Diameter. I would recommend the cylinder roller, as it is of the greatest importance to have a good cylinder, cast smooth and solid.

All the lard runs over this cylinder and is cooled off rapidly. This appliance is also of the greatest importance in amalgamating the different ingredients so that they are not apt to separate in hot weather. From the cylinder the lard will drop into

VII. A Box, under which a pump is placed, and from this box it is pumped into

VIII. The Lard Cooler.

The reason for pumping the stock into the cooler and not letting it drop direct from the cylinder roller into it, is that by pumping it we get rid of all lumps, and have only a smooth lard. This process has been arrived at after spending thousands of dollars in experiments to find out how to get rid of lumpy lard.

From the agitator the lard is run into the different packages, scales being placed on an adjustable platform. The packages to be filled are placed on the scales, and when filled are set aside to cool.

When fitting up a refinery or packing house, it is all important to have all piping, iron and brass fittings, valves, steam fittings, etc., the best that can be had.

RECIPE NO. 15

HOW TO PACK LARD

A great many refiners find, after packing their lard from the agitator in tubs and other packages, that, when they examine it the next morning, it has caved in in the middle and is badly cracked. This has caused them considerable trouble.

This inconvenience can be remedied by allowing the lard to cool slowly. When drawing the lard from the agitator it is usually placed in a freezing temperature, and this, as a rule, will cause the lard to crack and sink down in the middle.

Lard should be drawn off thick and allowed to cool in a temperature of about 36 degrees Fahrenheit.

SIZES OF PACKAGES USED

For the United States the packages in general use are:

        Tierces
        Buckets
        Tubs
        Tins
and **Fancy Tubs Grained.**

The tins are termed

    3-lb. Tins
    5-lb. Tins
    10-lb. Tins
    20-lb. Tins
    50-lb. Tins.

In summer a summer cover is put on over them with a crimping machine, so that they can be shipped to hot climates and not leak.

This crimping machine is most important and all those who do any shipping of lard should have one, as by its operation the packages are made air-tight. No solder is used; the package is crimped air-tight and the cover easily removed.

Next come the Ash Tubs. Ash tubs are sold in assorted sizes by the car lot; they generally run in the following sizes:

10 lbs.	50 lbs.
15 lbs.	55 lbs.
20 lbs.	60 lbs.
25 lbs.	80 lbs.
30 lbs.	Very few 80-lb. Tubs
35 lbs.	are now used.

Next come what are called Fancy Tubs. These are considered very pretty packages. They run in all sizes from 10 lbs. to 80 lbs.

These are the principal small packages used.

Tierces averaging about 340 lbs. net, Barrels of 200 lbs. and Half-Barrels of 125 lbs. are also used to a very large extent.

RECIPE NO. 16

HOW TO PUT A CRIMP ON LARD TO IMITATE A PURE KETTLE LEAF LARD

This has been experimented upon at a great expense of time and money. Indeed, it has been extremely difficult to obtain a regular, uniform result, but it has been finally reached and here is the process in full.

We all know that a pure kettle lard, if properly drawn, has a rough top to it, while all other lards are smooth-topped. We have discovered how a prime steam lard can be brought up to the same condition. The process is very simple.

When making a pure lard like silver leaf, in order to make it appear like a pure kettle leaf lard you must draw it direct from the receiver. It must not be cooled, but run into the packages at about 160 degrees Fahrenheit. Then you spread the packages well, so that plenty of air may pass between them and allow the lard to cool as quickly as possible.

It must not be moved or jarred. It must be left perfectly quiet and cooled quickly; it will then be found white, firm and beautiful, and will have the desired *rough top*.

I would recommend, when making this grade of lard, and in case you make your own steam lard, that you should always mix as much back fat as you can spare with your steam lard. This will make this brand a highly flavored lard, and you can always command for it a high price and brand it "Pure Lard," with a guarantee.

Just here I would make a suggestion as to the name to be chosen for this imitation of pure leaf lard. It will be found highly advantageous to work into the name the word "leaf," as the consumer will always have greater confidence in a brand that is called "leaf." "Silver Leaf," "Gold Leaf," "Maple Leaf," are all good names, as they convey to the consumer the idea they are getting *leaf lard*, and, therefore, something that is certainly pure. "*A Word to the Wise is Sufficient.*"

RECIPE NO. 17

TEMPERATURE AT WHICH LARD SHOULD BE PUMPED THROUGH THE FILTER

The temperature is

For Lard Compound, 200 to 210 degrees Fahrenheit

For Choice Family Lard, the same

For Silver Leaf Lard, about 180 degrees Fahrenheit

RECIPE NO. 18

HOW TO FIT UP A FILTER SO THAT IT CAN BE READILY CLEANED WITHOUT THE LOSS OF A PARTICLE OF LARD

In the first place, the filter should be set on blocks just high enough to allow the trough to be 4 inches higher than the refining kettle. This kettle should be set up through the floor about one foot. The tank will be about one foot up. The filter is on blocks, so as to be a little higher than the tank. The reason for this is that, when you start pumping through the filter, at first the stock will be a little "off" color. This portion of the stock must not, of course, be allowed into the receiver, but must run back into the refining tank until the color is right. The trough of the filter must be so arranged that when you first start filtering, the stock will run from the trough into the refining tank. When the stock is clear and of the right color, a cock is shut off, and it runs into the receiver under the filter.

Here is a diagram of the connections. One cock is close to the trough, the other opens and shuts the pipe that leads to the receiver. Now, the one opening the way to the receiver is not turned open until the lard is of a proper color and all right. On the contrary, the lard is allowed to run back into the refining kettle or tank until it is satisfactory; and if it should be

TROUGH UNDER FILTER

TO REFINING TANK

TO THE RECEIVER

too long in assuming the proper color, all you have to do is to add a little more fuller's earth. By the above arrangement it is never necessary to have any bad or off color lard, for you can keep on refining it until the color comes out right; when it is finally of the proper color, you turn off the cock that connects the trough with the tank, and turn on the cock that connects with the receiver.

The filter must be so arranged that you can pump through, first the refined lard, then the air, then the steam, and to do this you rig up your filter and pump.

Use pipe no smaller than one and one-half inch in diameter. The down pipe is the one coming from the refining kettle or tank, and the lard is pumped from the bottom up through the filter. When the tank is empty the pump is stopped and this cock is turned off. Of course the filter will then be full of lard. Now to save this you open the air-cock, start your air-pump and pump until all the lard is out of the filter; this will take say ten to fifteen minutes. When no more lard comes with the air blower, you turn this cock off and open your steam. But be sure before opening the steam to change the cocks on the trough, for if you don't do so, water will get mixed with the lard. Have your trough provided with a 2-inch hole at each end. When pumping through the filter close the one end and let the stock run into the receiver. When you start steaming shut this off and open the other end, to which a pipe is attached going through the floor; a barrel is to be placed underneath to catch the water and lard.

After the steam has done its work—and it must be kept on until no more lard is in the filter—nothing but the fuller's earth being left in the filter, then the steam is shut off, the filter opened and the fuller's earth drops out by shaking the cloths; a wooden scraper is used to clean what little of it is left on the cloths. The earth is of no value after being steamed. The cloths can be used three or four times. It is well to have two or three sets of cloths and always to use a clean set whenever making a change of formula. For instance, a lard compound having just been run through it will not do to put a silver leaf through the same cloths. But if you are running two or three runs of compound in succession it is all right to use the same set of cloths, provided, of course, that they are properly cleaned with steam after each run and the old fuller's earth shaken out.

All pipes should be so arranged as to have drain cocks. Always be sure to drain your pipes; otherwise they will soon be blocked. Have no L's put in, but T's at all turns, with plugs, so that if you do get blocked, you can clear your pipes without having to take them all down. By fitting up the filter as explained herein there should not be one particle of loss of stock, since the steam should be kept on until there is no more grease at all mixed with the fuller's earth.

RECIPE NO. 19

AT WHAT TEMPERATURE LARD SHOULD GO OVER THE ROLLER

Lard should go over the roller at a temperature of 120 degrees Fahrenheit, but if you are rushed, it may go over much hotter. Of course the hotter it goes over the more cold water you will have to use.

A good way to do, if time allows, is to run your lard in the afternoon and to leave it in the receiver over night, and the next morning run it over the roller. By so doing you will save a great deal of water. Be sure, in leaving the lard over night, that it does not grow too cold so that it will be stiff in the morning, for it must remain in a liquid state, so that it will run out of the receiver readily.

In large packing houses they have not the time to hold their lard, but refine it all day and run it over the rollers continuously; but then they have ice-machines and use brine for cooling the roller. In smaller packing houses it is better to hold it over night if you can.

RECIPE NO. 20

AT WHAT TEMPERATURE WATER SHOULD GO INTO THE ROLLER

The water in the roller should be at least 36 degrees Fahrenheit. Now, to obtain this temperature in summer if you have no brine, put a large tank on the floor above the roller; fill it with ice and salt; let this briny water gravitate down through the roller and run into a tank below, then have a pump rigged up and pump the liquid back into the upper tank; thus you obtain cold water and use it over and over again, gaining more water all the time by the melting of the ice. It will surprise you how fast the ice disappears when running this contrivance in summer. Therefore, if you have time and receivers enough, it will pay you to keep your lard over night and run it the next morning.

RECIPE NO. 21

AT WHAT TEMPERATURE TO DRAW LARD FROM THE AGITATOR

Lard compound or choice family lard should not be drawn from the agitator until it has got to such a point that it is thick. Then only should it be drawn into packages.

RECIPE NO. 22

SPECIAL TABLES FOR FIGURING HARDNESS FOR DIFFERENT CLIMATES

Here are a number of tables that will enable you to figure up the hardness necessary for different climates, so that after reaching warm or cold countries the lard will be of a proper texture, thus securing its prompt sale.

In figuring this you must take into consideration first, the hardness of the ingredients to be used.

Lard-stearine is twice as hard as Lard
Tallow is a grade harder than Lard
Oleo-stearine is three times as hard as Lard
Cotton Oil and Lard take care of themselves.

Now, for instance, we prepare a formula of, say

        40 per cent Lard
        20 per cent Cotton Oil
        20 per cent Tallow
        20 per cent Oleo-stearine
        ―――
        100 per cent.

How does this compare in hardness with lard? For, of course, in figuring we take lard as the basis of hardness.

Now— 40 Lard = 40 Lard
20 Oil = 20 Oil
───
60 per cent.

20 Tallow...... 1 time = 20
20 Oleo-stearine, 3 times = 60
───
80 per cent.

Now take 80 per cent
Less 60 per cent
───
Balance, 20 per cent.... This shows the product made according to this formula is *20 per cent Harder than Lard.*

Now take a formula of
75 per cent Oil
25 per cent Oleo-stearine
───
100 per cent

The 75 per cent of oil stands; figure the hardness of the 25 per cent of oleo-stearine

25 × 3 = 75 per cent Hardness
now subtract from 75 per cent Oil
the 75 per cent Extra-hardness
───
Balance, 00 per cent..... This shows

that a formula of 75 per cent oil and 25 per cent oleo-stearine would make a product exactly equal to lard itself in hardness.

A formula of say 80 per cent oil
5 per cent Oleo-stearine
15 per cent Tallow
---
100 per cent

would be figured as follows:

5 × 3 Oleo-stearine 15 per ct.   80 per ct. Oil
15 Tallow......15 ⅌ct. Deduct 30 per cent
---
30 per ct. Bal. 50 per cent.

This shows the product from this formula to be 50 per cent softer than lard.

Compound lard should always be softer than prime steam lard in winter, and such a formula of *50 per cent Softer than Lard* is all right for winter; in summer a formula of *30 per cent Harder than Lard* would be all right.

The best formulas for a lard that will not crumble can be easily figured out by following the above tables. A lard that is t ebo shipped to a warm climate should, of course, be *harder than prime steam lard* and one that is destined for a cold climate, *softer than prime steam lard.* Be sure to always find out where the product is to be shipped before you manufacture it according to this or that formula.

RECIPE NO. 23

EUROPEAN FORMULAS

The European lards are generally made from formulas composed of pure lard only

Their summer formula is:

      80 lbs. Prime Steam
      20 lbs. Lard-stearine

Total, 100 lbs.

In cooler weather less lard stearine is used.

There is also some demand for compound lard and this is made according to the price it is to be sold for. I might insert herein a number of formulas but, after all, the lards are to be made in accordance with the prices they sell for. Taking as a basis compound lard, choice family, etc., you just change the ingredients, either adding more of the higher-priced grade or reducing the quantity of the said grade and adding some of the lower-priced grade, such as tallow, cotton oil and deodorized greases. Of course this is easily figured out.

RECIPE NO. 24

BEST MODES OF RENDERING TALLOW WITH STEAM

Have a tank strong enough to stand a pressure of 90 lbs. working pressure to the square inch; put into this tank your rough fat and add a little water; then turn on steam and cook for about nine hours with 60 or 70 lbs. pressure. You will then produce a fine tallow, dry and hard, and one that will bring a better price for lard purposes than a low-cooked tallow, for it will have the flavor of prime steam lard. Being well cooked, the fibers will impregnate the tallow with this desirable odor, especially when using it in compound lard.

RECIPE NO. 25

HOW TO HARDEN TALLOW

To harden tallow, use for every 100 lbs. tallow a mixture of

> One-half lb. Sulphuric Acid
> One-half lb. Nitric Acid.

Melt the tallow and stir continuously, then run the above mixture into it slowly; then allow to settle. Draw off the acid water and wash well with clear water.

This will make a white, odorless tallow; of course there will be quite a good deal of gas developed, which must be carried off through a large pipe or hood placed over the tank whenever the stock is being treated in this way.

RECIPE NO. 26

HOW TO BLEACH TALLOW

Take the tallow to be bleached and put it into the refining tank; melt it and heat it up to 220 degrees Fahrenheit. Add from 7 to 10 per cent of fuller's earth to the tallow, allowing the blower or air-pump to agitate the stock thoroughly. When the fuller's earth has been added, start the tallow through the filter; then cool and pack as desired.

MACHINERY REQUIRED FOR MAKING OLEOMARGARINE

This machinery is to include:

1st. Wooden Tanks to put the fat in at the earliest moment after it has been taken from the animal; in these tanks the fat is washed and thoroughly chilled to eliminate all of the animal heat; from there it is taken to

2d. A Hasher.

3d. A Jacket Tank with an Agitator; then settled and allowed to run into

4th. Settling Tanks; then into

5th. Coolers on Wheels.

6th. Then into the seeding room and allowed to grain; then placed in cloths and put into

7th. Presses, to be pressed.

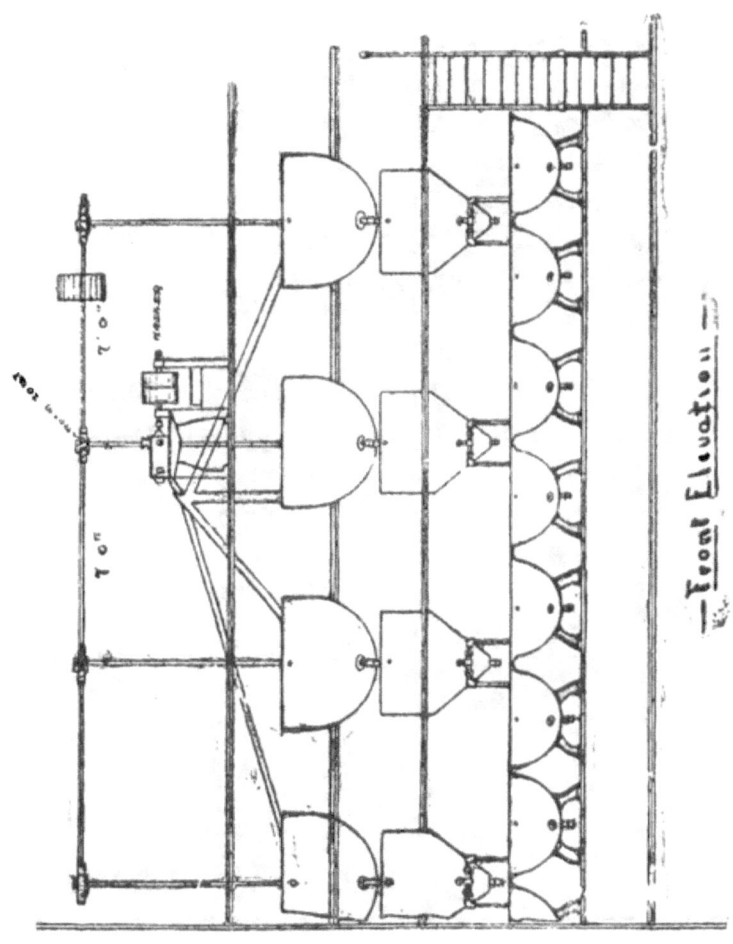

— Front Elevation —

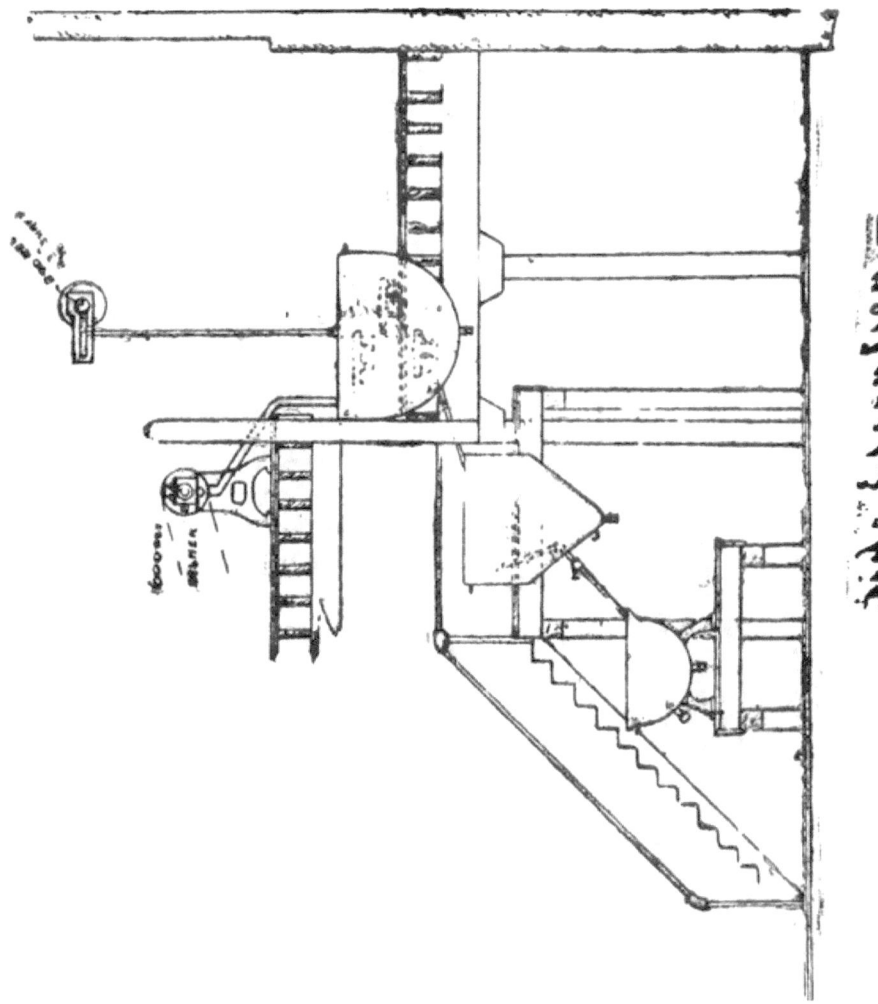

Side Elevation

RECIPE NO. 27

SELECTION AND PREPARATION OF FATS FOR OLEOMARGARINE

The selection and care of the fats are among the most important points in the manufacturing of oleomargarine, oleo-butter or butterine.

The best fats for making a No. 1 oil, such as is in great demand abroad, are obtained from the fat of cattle which is termed "long fat." No mutton fat must be used.

The moment the animal is killed, the fat should be put into water and thoroughly washed, the animal heat being thus taken out. Fat left lying about, even for two hours only, will not make a first-class oil.

RECIPE NO. 28.

HOW TO MANUFACTURE OLEOMARGARINE, OLEO-OIL, OLEO-BUTTER AND BUTTERINE

The first step after the fat has been cleaned, washed and thoroughly chilled, so that no animal heat remains, is to take it and cut it up into small pieces about the size of the hand.

It is then put in a hasher, so that all the fibres and tissues shall be torn asunder.

From this hasher it drops into an agitating jacket kettle, where it is heated to about 130 degrees Fahrenheit, no more. It is then allowed to remain in this kettle until it is melted and settled.

In settling, use large quantities of coarse salt.

After it is settled, it is drawn off into settling jackets, where it is allowed to settle still more, being heated so as to stand at a temperature of about 120 degrees Fahrenheit.

After being again well settled, it is drawn off into coolers on wheels.

Never allow this stock to run direct into the coolers, but run it through the finest hair-sieves you can obtain. The reason for this is that when melting fat at such a low temperature, there will always be found suspended small fibers or tissues; these, not being thoroughly cooked, are apt to get into the oil, and if they do get into it they will decompose and thus spoil a lot of stock. Be very careful on this point, as it is surprising what a very little it takes to spoil an otherwise excellent oil.

After the stock is run into these coolers on wheels it is wheeled into what is called the seeding room. The temperature in this room must be kept at from 75 to 80 degrees Fahrenheit. Never allow the thermometer in this room to vary much from these figures Here the stock is allowed to remain from 24 to 30 hours, when it will be found to have granulated and look very much like granulated sugar; it will form a solid mass with oil interspersed; the solid parts is crystallized stearine. When the stock has this appearance it is ready for the press. It is then filled into cloths, set in molds, wrapped up and put into the press to be pressed by a gradually increasing pressure, under which the oil is extracted, leaving the oleo-stearine in the cloths.

This press-room should have a temperature of about 89 to 92 degrees Fahrenheit.

If the fat has been properly handled from the

start, a clear, yellow, sweet oil is pressed and this oil is what is termed Oleomargarine-oil or Butter-oil.

Now, when oleo-butter is to be made, this oil is taken and cooled to about 70 degrees Fahrenheit.

About 100 lbs. of the oil, with about 15 to 20 lbs. of sour milk, are placed in a churn. Two and a half ounces of solution of Annetto, containing one-half to three-fourths of an ounce of solution of bicarbonate of soda, may then be added to the whole; then it is at once run into a tank on wheels, containing pounded ice, the mess running into the ice and being continually mixed with shovels or pitchforks until sufficiently cooled and chilled. Generally one man on each side of the tank is used to mix the stock well through the pounded ice.

By this process the grain is completely broken, and the butter will be as smooth as desired.

After remaining in contact with the ice for 2 or 3 hours, it is then dumped on an inclined table and crumbled up, so that all the ice will melt out. Then about 30 lbs. at a time are put into a churn, with 20 to 25 lbs. of sour milk, and the whole is churned for about 15 minutes.

By this last process the flavor and odor desired are imparted to the butter; then the working, draining and salting (three-fourths of an ounce of salt to the pound), complete the manufacturing.

EUROPEAN PROCESSES FOR MANUFACTURING OLEOMARGARINE, ETC.

An account of the most recent European processes for manufacturing oleomargarine, etc., is here in order.

Those processes consist:

1st. In washing the fat.
2d. In crystallizing the fat.
3d. In pressing the crystallized fat.
4th. In churning with cotton oil, etc., and milk.

The fresh suet is first freed from all adhering tissues and is then thrown into large tubs, wherein the blood is carefully washed off by means of cold water.

It is then put through a meat hasher, where it is cut and drawn up into a white mass, which is delivered into a kettle jacketed with warm water and supplied with a stirring apparatus. Here it is warmed up to 122 degrees Fahrenheit with constant agitation for two hours.

The stirring is then stopped, water is introduced and the rendered fat is forced through a pipe into the jacketed tub. From there it is drawn into small trays, and in 24 hours it is cooled down to 80 degrees Fahrenheit, when it is wrapped in cloths and put in a hydraulic press, and the oleomargarine (a mixture of stearine, palmatine and oleoine) is squeezed out of it.

The oleomargarine oil is then put into a churn, together with milk, cotton oil and a little butter color. In fifteen minutes the churning is completed. The churned mass is then worked in the same manner as butter, to remove the milk and water.

Artificial butter, thus carefully prepared, will keep for months without becoming rancid.

CHEMICAL COMPARISON BETWEEN OLEO-BUTTER AND NATURAL BUTTER

A natural butter contains:

	FAT	CASEINE	ASH	WATER
Good quality	86.06	0.42	0.12	13.77
Poor to bad	82.60	0.72	0.20	17.08
Fresh Hay Butter	70.19	2.59	0.25	26.19
Common Cow Butter	86.06	0.40	0.14	13.77

An oleo-butter contains:

	FAT	CASEINE	ASH	WATER
Oleomargarine-butter	86.24	1.20	....	12.56
Other brands of Oleo	87.15	0.57	1.63	15.50

RECIPE NO. 29

TO PREPARE THE LEAF FOR MAKING NEUTRAL

Take the leaf lard and hang it in a cold place; allow it to hang for 24 hours, so that all the animal heat is taken out. In hanging great care must be taken not to allow the leaf to overlap, as it will prevent the animal heat from leaving it. The pieces must be hung up smooth and not allowed to touch one another.

RECIPE NO. 30

HOW TO MANUFACTURE WET AND DRY NEUTRAL

The leaf, after being thoroughly cooled, so that no more animal heat remains in it, is taken and hashed and melted at a low temperature, not over 160 degrees Fahrenheit. There it is treated in about the same manner as when manufacturing oleo. It is then allowed to settle and is run into another jacket tank. It now being freed from all fibers and tissues, it is heated to 200 degrees Fahrenheit. From this jacket it is run into small tanks of strong brine holding about 500 pounds.

It is allowed to remain in this water for twelve hours. A small percentage of nitric acid has been added to this water to deodorize the lard. The next day the plug is pulled out and the water let off; then fresh water is added and the stock well stirred and washed, so as to wash out of it all the acid water. It is generally allowed to remain in fresh water over night, always keeping the water cold.

Wet Neutral is drained and packed, and sold with a certain amount "off" for the water.

Dry Neutral.—To manufacture same, the wet neutral stock is placed in a jacket and very slowly heated, not over 110 degrees Fahrenheit. Then it is allowed to settle, the water is drawn off, and the stock is drawn into tierces for shipment.

Always draw the neutral, to ship it, when it is as *cold* as possible; never do so when it is hot or warm; be sure that it is *cold*.

RECIPES NOS. 31, 32 AND 33

LATEST AND MOST APPROVED MODES OF CARING FOR BONES, BLOOD AND OFFAL

No 31. The Bones are dried and sold for different purposes. The jaw-bones and skulls are sold to sugar refiners, who use them for filtering molasses and syrups; they grind them and burn them.

The shin-bones are put in cold water over night, the water soaking in and causing the marrow to leave the bones. They are then washed in warm water and a little sal soda is added to whiten the bones. Never boil the water; just warm it enough so that it will not scald your hand. After the bones are in the water a few hours, they are cleaned and put away to dry. These bones are used for making brush-handles, knife-handles, etc., and are always in demand at a good price.

No. 32. Blood is caught in a tank, where open steam is put into it and it is allowed to cook until it thickens, stirring it occasionally until it coagulates. It is then taken out, put into bags and pressed. Then it is put into an

Anderson Drier until it is thoroughly dried, when it is removed and spread on the floor until all the heat is out. Finally, it is packed into sacks and stored or shipped ready for market.

No. 33. The Offal is tanked and cooked for six hours; it is then skimmed and what fat can be gathered is saved. It is then drained, pressed and dried. This product, after being dried, is termed "Tankage Fertilizer." The dried blood is termed "Blood Tankage," and is worth considerably more than the former for making fertilizer. Both are analyzed before being bougnt, and are sold at so much per unit of ammonia. Both blood and offal should be worked up as soon as possible, so as not to allow either to decompose, as, by decomposing, they deteriorate in value and lose their strength of ammonia.

RECIPE NO. 34

PURIFICATION AND BLEACHING OF FATTY ACIDS

Sulphuric acid is used for this process; for example:

Three quarters to one and a half per cent of the oil of vitriol will precipitate the mucilage and other matters; first it removes the water by which these substances were held in solution by the oil, and afterward clears the mucous matters themselves and renders them insoluble by effecting their destruction. A lead-lined tank is used, and also an open steam coil. The stock should be cooked about one hour and then allowed to settle.

BEST GRADE OF COTTON SEED OIL

The best grade of cotton seed oil to be used is that which has a light color, is free from any odor, and is called "Butter Oil."

Refined cotton oil has a specific gravity of 0.9264 at 59 degrees Fahrenheit.

RECIPE NO. 35

HOW TO ADULTERATE OILS

Use neutral oil. This is used by nearly all compounders and mixers of oil. A good neutral oil will stand a cold test of between 20 and 30 degrees above zero, Fahrenheit; there are, of course, different grades. The light colored oil is from 33 to 34 specific gravity; the dark oil from 31 to 32. There is no fixed rule regarding the use of these oils for mixing with animal oils. Some use 5 gallons to a barrel of animal oil, such as lard oil; some use 10 gallons, and I have used, myself, as much as 15 gallons to the barrel, and I have known as much as 20 gallons to be used, or, in other words, 30 gallons of lard oil and 20 gallons of neutral oil. I consider 20 per cent a good mixture; and I think a lard oil, for some purposes, mixed to this extent is even better than in its pure state, as the neutral oil will have a tendency to prevent corrosion of metal, while, of course, it cheapens the cost of lard oil.

The dark neutral oil is used by a great many in mixing vegetable oils, such as linseed, etc.

In the matter of the adulteration of oils, my experience has shown me that firms carry the adulteration just as far as their consciences will permit them. There is no set rule to follow.

RECIPE NO. 36

HOW TO ARRANGE CATCH-BASINS SO AS TO AVOID LOSS OF GREASE IN WASHING FLOORS

Have one large tank built, and set it in the ground, allowing everything from the floors to be washed into it. This tank is to be arranged as shown in the following cut.

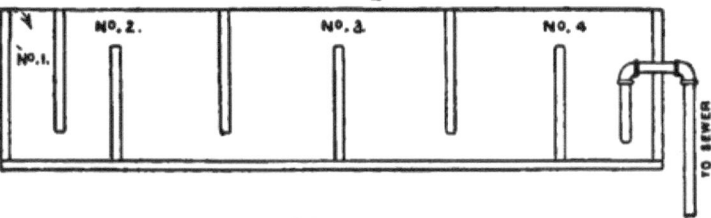

Into No. 1 everything runs; the water will run under the trap into No. 2; over No. 2 into the next compartment, etc., etc., until it reaches the last space; here it runs up through a 2-inch pipe, set in so that it only goes within 2 inches of the bottom of the tank; the grease, being the lighter, will always be on top of the water, and will almost always be found in the first and second sections. Should some of it, however, get out, it will positively be caught in the other sections, and it is impossible for any grease to get out of the tank by this arrangement.

RECIPE NO. 37

FREE ACID TESTS

For these tests use an 8-ounce bottle; put in it 2 ounces of alcohol; add a few drops of tamarick (tamarisk) to color the solution. It should color the alcohol red. Place the bottle in hot water and heat it to about 150 degrees Fahrenheit, and then add to this alcohol 10 cubic centimeters of the oil to be treated. Shake well. The mixture should now be yellow. Take from a burette a caustic potash solution, and run it very slowly from the burette into this 8-ounce bottle; it must get into the mixture drop by drop, shaking well after every few drops, until it turns red—a nice cherry red—which color must remain permanent. Now look at the burette and read off how many cubic centimeters of the caustic potash solution it took to cause this reaction. Divide the figure by two and you will have the percentage of free acid in the article being tested. Now, at the first reading, it seems as if only a chemist could do this properly, but let me say that the operation is as simple as it is important.

All you have to do is to go to a chemist or to a drug store and tell them that you want two quarts of 95 degrees alcohol, to which an eighth ounce of dry carbonate of soda has been added, and that you want also one quart of caustic potash solution of sufficient strength to allow 31½ cubic centimeters of it to exactly neutralize 5 cubic centimeters of the above mixture of acid, sulphuric and water, which contains 49 milligrams, or 1.2504 per cubic centimeter. This will give you the solution to work with.

Buy one *pipette* of 10 cubic centimeters, one *burette* of 30 c c., and 2 ounces of tamarick.

You take all this to your office and begin making your test. Take an 8-ounce bottle. Into this put 2 ounces of the alcohol; you then place this in hot water or hold it over a spirit lamp and heat it to about 150 degrees Fahrenheit, or until it feels warm to your hand; next you heat the oil to be treated to about the same temperature. You put your pipette into this oil and suck up to the mark 10 c. c. on the pipette; when you have reached it exactly, put your finger on the end you had in your mouth and this will prevent the oil from running out. Look at it carefully and if there is not enough put in more; if there is too much, let the surplus drop back into the oil until the pipette marks exactly 10 c. c.

When you have got this, put the other end into the 8-ounce bottle containing the alcohol and tamarick, remembering that the 2 ounces alcohol must receive from ten to fifteen drops of tamarick to color it. I generally use this amount to color the alcohol.

Now let this oil run into the alcohol and tamarick mixture. Shake it well and it will turn out a nice, bright yellow. Now you take your burette into which you have put the caustic potash preparation. The burette is marked off in tenths—mark where you start. Suppose it shows 30 c. c. of potash. You allow a few drops of this to pass into the 8-ounce bottle with the oil, alcohol and tamarick solution. Shake it well; if it does not remain a bright cherry red put in a few more drops, shaking the bottle continually until the mixture remains a bright cherry red. This then finishes the process.

You then look at your burette and find out how many cubic centimeters of the potash solution have been used. If you used 4 c. c., divide this by 2 and your oil will be known to contain 2 per cent of free acid. If you have used 6 c. c. of the potash solution, your oil contains 3 per cent of free acid, and so on.

A good lard oil should not run over 2 per cent of free acid, and some will go as low down as 1 per cent. Other oils run higher, some as high as 20 per cent of free acid, but these are termed No. 2 and No. 3 lard oils.

RECIPE NO. 3

DELICATE METHOD OF OBTAINING THE PERCENTAGE OF STEARIC ACID OR OLEIC ACID CONTAINED IN TALLOW, GREASES, ETC.

The following process is the one used in most laboratories. It is not a difficult one, but must be closely carried out as directed. As most of the tallow is now bought and paid for according to the percentage of stearic acid it contains, it is important to know how to make a test.

Good, fine tallow will contain the following proportions:

> 45 per cent Stearic Acid
> 45 per cent Oleine Oil, or Red Oil
> 8 per cent Glycerine
> 2 per cent lost in manufacturing
> ———
> 100 per cent.

To test tallow so as to ascertain the point of crystallization or solidification, *the following apparatus and substances* are needed:

1st. A suitable vessel, basin-shaped, and capable of holding about 2 quarts or 2 liters of liquid. A copper vessel preferred, but it must be of such material as will resist the chemical action of acids.

Suitable means of heating the above must be procured.

2d. A pair of scales is needed, capable of weighing 50 grams of tallow, or a pipette capable of measuring said quantity.

3d. A graduated glass is to be used, capable of measuring from 1 to 60 cubic centimeters.

4th. We need, besides, a pipette of about 1 to 200 cubic centimeter capacity, with rubber ball attached for sucking up liquid from the solution of water and fatty acid.

5th. Also a thermometer of the finest grade, capable of registering up to 100 Centigrade or 500 degrees Fahrenheit, each degree being divided into fifths and tenths.

6th. One half-dozen test tubes about 5 inches long and about three-fourths to seven-eighths of an inch in diameter.

7th. A frame of iron or wood, or of any suitable material, for suspending the thermometer over and into one of the test-tubes; the latter is to be held in position by a bottle of suitable size by means of a hole cut in a cork, as shown in the illustration herein inserted.

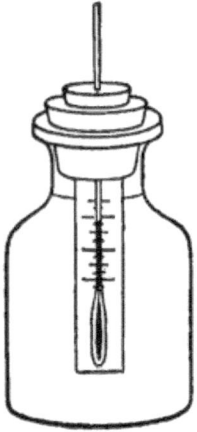

8th. About 2 quarts of caustic soda, a solution of 36 degrees Beaume strength; about 2 quarts of sulphuric acid, a solution of 36 degrees Beaume strength; about 2 quarts of alcohol.

9th. A glass rod for stirring.

Here is the *Testing Operation:*

Weigh or measure 50 grams of the sample of tallow to be tested, and heat it in the vessel until it begins to smoke. But care must be used not to allow it to burn.

Now add 40 cubic centimeters of the caustic soda solution, and 35 cubic centimeters of alcohol. Stir this until it forms into a paste, then add slowly about one quart of boiling water, and boil until thoroughly saponified, an operation which will take but a few minutes. Then pour in a little cold water to cool the solution, and boil until it becomes perfectly clear and the fatty acid separates from the soap. This last operation will occupy one hour—more or less.

The water must now be drawn off by means of a pipette, and a sufficient quantity of the fat remaining, or of the fatty acids, be put in one of the test-tubes and suspended in a bottle by means of a cork with a hole cut in, and fitted into the neck of said bottle as shown in drawing.

Place the bulb of the thermometer into one of the test-tubes, and see that the bulb is entirely covered by the liquid fatty acids, as near the center as possible.

The thermometer must be suspended so as to swing freely from the frame of iron or wood. The temperature of the fatty acid should be sufficiently high to secure a complete liquefaction at, say about 55 to 70 degrees Centigrade.

Watch the thermometer carefully; it can be read accurately by means of a small magnifying glass. As the mercury descends and finally approaches the point of crystallization, it will move more slowly and finally stop.

After a while it will rise. As soon as it stops falling and crystals begin to appear around the bulb, stir with the bulb of the thermometer the matter inside the tube, three or four times to the right and as many times to the left, then let it stand in the tube as near the center as possible, and begin watching more closely than ever.

The mercury in the thermometer will rise steadily, and the highest point it reaches is the crystallization point. The thermometer should be protected against currents of air and kept perfectly still.

RECIPE NO. 39

HOW TO COOL A MEAT MARKET WITH BRINE CIRCULATION

Here is a nice and economical way of keeping your market fairly cool:

Have plenty of 1 ¼ inch pipe placed about 6 or 7 feet above the level of your floor. Have *above* this floor, a large tank built and well insulated; in this tank place your ice and salt, keeping the tank well covered. This will reduce the temperature of the water to 32 degrees Fahrenheit; then open a valve and let this water flow through your pipes and run into a tank built *under* your floor.

This second tank, of course, must also be well insulated and so arranged that ice and salt can be put into it; then a pump is arranged in connection with this tank, and the same water is pumped back, upstairs, into Tank No. 1. If you keep the doors of your store closed and use a little care, you can keep your temperature down to 55 or 60 degrees Fahrenheit, in hot weather, and do so very cheaply. Of course the temperature can be brought down even lower by using more ice and salt and plenty of iron piping, and by insulating your shop thoroughly.

RECIPE NO. 40

HOW TO KEEP AND USE A CHILL-ROOM TO BEST ADVANTAGE

A chill-room should be filled every alternate day.

Hogs are to hang 40 to 43 hours and cattle the same.

Hogs should hang in a temperature of 32 degrees Fahrenheit.

Cattle should hang in a temperature of 38 degrees Fahrenheit.

Hogs averaging 200 to 250 lbs. require, each, 3½ sq. ft. of space.

Cattle of 800 lbs. dressed, require, each, from 10 to 12 sq. ft. of space.

To chill 1,000 hogs and 300 cattle will require a machine of 100 tons refrigerating capacity; storage will take besides 40 to 50 tons; you therefore need two machines of 80 tons each, and they will cost you, complete, about $40,000.

In figuring what storage is required, always figure 8,000 to 12,000 cubic feet per ton refrigerator.

RECIPE NO. 41

HOW TO PROPERLY FIT UP A TEST ROOM

Every lard refinery or packing house should fit up a small room, kept under lock and key, for making tests, etc. In this room should be made all tests of lards, tallows, oils, greases, etc. You need no professional chemist for those tests. You can very easily learn how to make yourselves the few occasional tests your business may require.

To fit up your little laboratory, go to any chemical supply shop and purchase:

3 12-ounce beakers
1 dozen 8-ounce bottles
1 10-c. c. pipette
2 glass funnels, 6 inches diameter
2 8-ounce wash-bottles
1 porcelain mortar and pestle of 4 inches diameter
1 Bunsen gas-lamp, plain
1 glass spatula, 6 inches long
1 iron ring stand
2 dozen test-tubes, 6 inches by ¾ inch
1 tube rack of 12 holes

1 chemical thermometer, 600 degrees Fahrenheit
3 evaporators of porcelain, 6 inches in diameter
3 evaporators of porcelain, 12 inches in diameter
1 package filter paper, 12 inches in diameter
2 rings for filter-stands
1 small tincture press.

These articles will cost but a trifle, and they will be sufficient for making a number of tests.

RECIPE NO. 42

HOW TO USE AND COMPARE THE DIFFERENT SCALES OF THERMOMETERS

When using thermometers, much annoyance has been caused by the existence of the three different scales in use in the different civilized countries of the world.

The *Reaumur Scale* prevails in Germany.

The *Centigrade* (or Celsius) *Scale*, in France and generally wherever the metric system of weights and measures is followed, and in all, except English-speaking countries, for every scientific purpose.

The *Fahrenheit Scale*, in the United States and the British Empire.

The best argument in favor of the *Centigrade Scale* is that it includes between 0 degree (freezing point of water) and 100 degrees (boiling point of water) all the temperatures generally met with in the civilized zone.

The *Fahrenheit Scale* is convenient on account of its short degrees, of which there are 180 between the freezing point of water (32 degrees) and the boiling point of water (212 degrees), thus allowing more minute calculations without the use of fractions. Its low zero makes it possible, in temperate climates, to dispense with the sign—.

The *Reaumur Scale* divides the space between the freezing and boiling of water into 80 degrees, instead of 100 degrees, as in the centigrade system.

The conversion of any one of these scales into another is very simple. You just proceed as follows:

1st. To convert a temperature given by a Fahrenheit scale into one given by a centigrade scale, subtract 32 from the figure on the Fahrenheit thermometer, multiply the remainder by 5 and divide by 9. The product will give you the same temperature in centigrade degrees.

2d. To convert Fahrenheit degrees into Reaumur degrees, subtract 32, multiply by 4 and divide by 9. The product gives you the same temperature according to the Reaumur scale.

3d. To convert centigrade degrees into Fahrenheit degrees, multiply the centigrade temperature by 9 and divide by 5, adding 32 to the result. You will then have the same temperature expressed in Fahrenheit degrees.

4th. To convert Reaumur degrees into Fahrenheit degrees, multiply the Reamur temperature by 9 and divide by 4, adding 32 to the result. You'll have the same temperature expressed in Fahrenheit degrees.

The following is a table giving equivalents in Centigrade, Reaumur and Fahrenheit degrees up to the boiling point of water, prepared for the convenience of those who do not care to take the trouble of converting temperatures from one scale into another.

COMPARISONS BETWEEN CENTIGRADE, REAUMUR AND FAHRENHEIT SCALES

C.	R.	F.	C.	R.	F.
−30	−24.0	−22.0	1	−0.8	30.2
−29	−23.0	−20.2	0	0.0	32.0
−28	−22.4	−18.4	1	0.8	33.8
−27	−21.6	−16.6	2	1.6	35.6
−26	−20.8	−14.8	3	2.4	37.4
−25	−20.0	−13.0	4	3.2	39.2
−24	−19.2	−11.2	5	4.0	41.0
−23	−18.4	−9.4	6	4.8	42.8
−22	−17.6	−7.6	7	5.6	44.6
−21	−16.8	−5.8	8	6.4	46.4
−20	−16.0	−4.0	9	7.2	48.2
−19	−15.2	−2.2	10	8.0	50.0
−18	−14.4	−0.4	11	8.8	51.8
−17	−13.6	1.4	12	9.6	53.6
−16	−12.8	3.2	13	10.4	55.4
−15	−12.0	5.0	14	11.2	57.2
−14	−11.2	6.8	15	12.0	69.0
−13	−10.4	8.6	16	12.8	60.8
−12	−9.6	10.4	17	13.6	62.6
−11	−8.8	12.2	18	14.4	64.4
−10	−8.0	14.0	19	15.2	66.2
−9	−7.2	15.8	20	16.0	68.0
−8	−6.4	17.6	21	16.8	69.8
−7	−5.6	19.4	22	17.6	71.6
−6	−4.8	21.2	23	18.4	73.4
−5	−4.0	23.0	24	19.2	75.2
−4	−3.2	24.8	25	20.0	77.0
−3	−2.4	26.6	26	20.8	78.8
−2	−1.6	28.4	27	21.6	80.6

COMPARISONS BETWEEN CENTIGRADE REAUMUR AND FAHRENHEIT SCALES

C.	R.	F.	C.	R.	F.
28	22.4	82.4	65	52.0	149.0
29	23.2	81.2	66	52.8	150.8
30	24.0	86.0	67	53.6	152.6
31	24.3	87.8	68	54.4	154.4
32	25.6	89.6	69	55.2	156.2
33	26.4	91.4	70	56.0	158.0
34	27.2	93.2	71	56.8	159.8
35	28.0	95.0	72	57.6	161.6
36	28.8	96.8	73	58.4	163.4
37	29.6	98.6	74	59.2	165.2
38	30.4	100.4	75	60.0	167.0
39	31.2	102.2	76	60.8	168 8
40	32.0	104.4	77	61.6	170.6
41	32.8	105.8	78	62.4	172.4
42	33.6	107.6	79	63.2	174.2
43	34.4	109.4	80	64.0	176 0
44	35.2	111.2	81	64.8	177.8
45	36.0	113.0	82	65.6	179 6
46	36.8	114.9	83	66.4	181.4
47	37.6	116.6	84	67.2	183.2
48	38.4	118.4	85	68.0	185.0
49	39.2	120.2	86	68.8	186.8
50	40.0	122.0	87	69.6	188.6
51	40.8	123.8	88	70.4	190.4
52	41.6	125.6	89	71.2	192.5
53	42.4	127.4	90	72.0	194.0
54	43.2	129.2	91	72.8	195.8
55	44.0	131.0	92	73.6	197.6
56	44.8	132.8	93	74.4	199.4
57	45.6	134.6	94	75.2	202.2
58	46.4	136.4	95	76.0	203.0
59	47.2	138.2	96	76.8	204.8
60	48.0	140.0	97	77.6	206.6
61	48.8	141.8	98	78.4	208.4
62	49.6	143.6	99	79.2	210.2
63	50.4	145.4	100	80.0	202.0
64	51.2	147.2			

RECIPE NO 43

SPECIFICATIONS FOR LARD OIL

Two grades of lard oil, known on the market as "Extra" and "Extra No. 1," are used, the former principally for burning, the other as a lubricant. The material desired under specifications is oil pressed from the lard of corn-fed hogs, unmixed with other oils and containing the least possible amount of free acid. Also, from October 1st to May 1st it should show a cold test of not higher than 43 degrees Fahrenheit. Oil from lard of "mash" or distillery-fed hogs does not give good results in service and should never be sent to railroads. Also care should be observed to have the oil made from fresh lard; old lard gives an oil that does not burn well and also works badly as a lubricant. Whenever pressing lard always figure 15 cents per 100 lbs. for labor.

The use of the so-called "neatsfoot stock," either alone or as an admixture in making the "Extra No. 1" grade, is not recommended. Neatsfoot oil is used by the railroad companies when the price will admit, but it is always preferred unmixed. Both grades of oil will be purchased on sample and shipments must conform to sample. A 4-ounce sample is sufficient and should be sent to the purchasing agent of the road; the color of the sample has an influence in the securing of orders; the lightest in color are always considered the best. Shipments must be made as soon as possible after the order is placed. All shipments received at any shop after October 1st will be subjected to cold tests and rejected if they fail, unless it can be shown that the shipment has been more than a week in transit.

The *extra* grade will not be accepted when

1st. It contains admixtures of any other oils.

2d. It contains more free acid than is neutralized by 4 c. c. of alkali, as described.

3d. It shows a cold test above 45 degrees Fahrenheit from October 1 to May 1.

A shipment of *Extra* No. 1 will not be accepted when

1st. It contains admixtures of any other oils.

2d. It contains more free acid than is neutralized by 30 c. c. of alkali.

3d. It shows a cold test above 45 degrees Fahrenheit from October 1 to May 1.

RECIPE NO 44.

PURE NEATSFOOT OIL

This oil is made from the feet only, by heating just below boiling point.

Then the feet are taken and screened; this throws out the meat, etc. This meat is then boiled thoroughly and allowed to settle, when the stock is carefully skimmed, and this oil makes a No. 1 neatsfoot oil.

Now, if this oil is taken and filtered, the floating stearine will be caught. It then sells for an extra oil. The stearine can be put into the tallow tank and used for tallow.

The head stock oil is refined and an A No. 1 oil made by pressing this stearine as it goes into the tallow-tank.

RECIPE NO. 45

COLD TEST OF LARD OILS

This test is made as follows:

A couple of ounces of oil are put in a 4-ounce sample bottle and a thermometer introduced in it. The oil is then frozen, a freezing mixture of ice and salt being used if necessary. When the oil has become hard, the bottle is removed from the freezing mixture and the frozen oil allowed to soften, being stirred and well mixed at the same time, by means of the thermometer, until the mass will run from one end of the bottle to the other.

The reading of the thermometer, when this operation has been gone through, is regarded as the cold test of the oil.

We have treated in our Recipe No. 37, under the heading of FREE ACID TESTS, all that concerns this important analysis.

SPECIFICATION ISSUED BY THE PENN. R. R. COMPANY POWER DEPARTMENT

"From this date all materials used as lubricants and burning oils will be purchased by weight, and quotation of prices and bills must be by the pound and not gallons. In quoting prices cents and 100ths should be used. A separate bill must be rendered for every shipment, however small, even though it be but a portion of the whole order; and the bill must be made as soon as possible after the shipment is made.

"Every package containing lubricants and burning oils must be plainly marked with the gross weight and tare.

"This applies to oil-tank cars as well as to barrels.

"Parties failing to mark both gross and tare on their packages must accept the company's weights without any question.

"Whenever a shipment of any lubricant or burning oil is received at any point, it will be immediately weighed and, when practicable, will be at once emptied and the empty packages weighed. If not practicable to empty all the packages, 5 per cent of the shipment will be emptied and the tares taken of the whole. The tares of the whole shipment will then be adjusted in accordance with the weight of the 5 per cent; if the net weight found from above data is less than the amount charged for in the bill by more than 1 per cent, a deduction will be made from the bill equal to the amount of deficiency over 1 per cent.

"This 1 per cent covers leakage in transit and the amount which adheres to the barrels when emptying them, also possible slight difference in scales."

ANALYSIS OF PRIME WINTER-STRAINED LARD OIL

Prime winter-strained lard oil contains less than 2 per cent of free acids, for the cold test must stand a temperature of 45 degrees Fahrenheit or less

Its specific gravity is 22 to 24 degrees Beaume, at a temperature of 60 degrees Fahrenheit.

SUNDRY RECOMMENDATIONS CONCERNING EXTRA WINTER STRAINED LARD OIL

In pressing stock to obtain E. W. S. (i. e., Extra Winter-Strained Lard Oil), always press from the choicest prime steam lard. There is always a good demand for the oil and stearine.

Press it in winter, on account of the cold temperature; in summer, if you have refrigerating facilities to keep the press-room cold, always make a test of your lard by pressing a small quantity in your laboratory in your tincture-press.

Make an acid test of your oil; this you can do by following directions under heading of *Free*

Acid Tests. If your oil shows *over* 2 per cent of acid, there is no use pressing it out of the lard you are just then working from, and expecting it to pass for an E. W. S. lard oil, as it is sure to be rejected. But if it shows 2 per cent of acid or *less*, press it and you will have no trouble getting top price for both oil and stearine.

RECIPE NO. 46

HOW TO DETECT WATER AND IMPURITIES

Water. Weigh carefully and exactly 20 grams of the article to be tested in a small porcelain dish; then place the latter over an alcohol stove; let it get very hot without burning it; when small bubbles cease coming to the top, reweigh, and the loss in weight will give you the percentage of water.

Impurities. Now take the material in a dish, and, after carefully weighing two filter papers against each other, add some naphtha to the material and pass the whole through one of the filter papers. Carefully wash all grease out of filter paper with warm naphtha, using a wash bottle. Weigh the two papers against each other again; the increased weight gained by the one you used for the above operation gives you the percentage of impurities. An oven may be used instead of an alcohol stove. Do not heat above 180 degrees Fahrenheit.

RECIPE NO. 47

BREAKFAST BACON

Is made by cutting the regular belly lengthwise, usual standard sold four to six pounds, well smoked, and may be canvased or uncanvased as desired for the market which it is intended for.

RECIPE NO. 48

BARREL BACKS

Backs shall be cut from the backs of heavy, well fatted hogs, after taking out full cut ribs and loins, each barrel containing a proper proportion of middle and other cuts, cut uniform in shape and as free from lean as practicable, and entirely free from bone. Packed five layers to the barrel, and weighing not less than two hundred pounds, with not less than forty pounds of good, coarse salt, when packed fresh from the block one hundred and ninety pounds of green meat to be weighed in.

RECIPE NO. 49

EXTRA PRIME PORK

Extra Prime Pork shall be made of heavy untrimmed shoulders, cut into three pieces, the leg to be cut off clean to the breast; to be packed one hundred and ninety pounds of green meat into each barrel, with the same quantity and quality of salt as Mess Pork.

RECIPE NO. 50

IRISH CUT SIDES

Irish Cut Sides should be made the same as Long Clears, with the knuckle bone left in. Packed in boxes to fit the meat, five hundred to six hundred pounds, in dry salt.

RECIPE NO. 51

LEAN ENDS

Lean ends shall be packed in the same manner as Backs, from well selected medium-weight bellies. Cut square at each end and pack five layers to the barrel.

RECIPE NO. 52

CLEAR PORK

Clear Pork shall be cut and packed in the same manner as Backs, except that the belly end shall be left on each strip; but every piece must be cut square at each end, and packed five layers to the barrel.

RECIPE NO. 53

COOPERAGE

All pork and lard shall be in new packages, i. e., packages never having been previously filled, unless otherwise stated at the time of sale, with the exception of lard sold in tubs, which may be second-hand tubs, but the packages must be clean, and in good order.

RECIPE NO. 54

MAKING SWEET PICKLE FOR CURING MEATS—HAMS

One tierce of 16-lb. hams contains about 16 to 19 pieces.

In packing these, put into the tierce with the hams

    18 ozs. Saltpeter
    4 lbs. Granulated Sugar

Then fill the tierce up with 85 degrees proof pickle for a mild cure.

It will take these hams 85 to 90 days to become cured.

When first packed they will weigh about 300 lbs. When taken out they will weigh about 322 lbs.

These hams should be kept in a temperature not over 38 degrees Fahrenheit and should be rolled the fifth day after being packed; again on the fifteenth day; then again on the thirtieth day; then allow them to rest. The object in rolling them is to find the cripples and leakers; also to evenly mix the ingredients and also to get the pickle into the hams that might partly be dry. Should you find leakers, be sure to have the tierce reopened and repickled. Always use the same strength of pickle as was used before.

RECIPE NO. 55

DRY SALTING MEATS

Use Ashten salt.

Get ready a barrel full of 100 degrees proof pickle.

Now take the meats, drop them into the pickle, take them out and put them in a salt-box and rub a little salt over them. Then pile them cuts *up*, flanks *up*, sprinkle 2 ounces fine saltpeter over the pile; shake a small handful of salt on top.

In packing hams lay them left and right, in order to allow the pickle to run down the stifle joint; then, in five days, overhaul them in a box.

Always try to save the pickle that these hams make and use this pickle on the hams again, then rub them slightly with salt and lay them on a pile. In about 10 days overhaul them again. If your temperature is steady, at, say from 36 to 38 degrees, you can let them stay fifteen days. Use fine salt again when overhauling them. You will find they have a fine cherry color, which suits the English market. They are ready to pack any time after the 25th day, as they cure in shipment.

RECIPE NO. 56

POINTS OF INTEREST ABOUT HAMS

In making hams, 12 to 14-lb. hams are worth more than hams 16 to 18 lbs.

Be sure to always save the pickle these hams make, as no pickle can be made to equal it.

Light, long clears, 35 to 40 lbs.

Cumberland light, about 32 lbs; heavy, 35 to 40 lbs.

Birmingham sides, light, about 35 to 40 lbs.

Yorkshire, 40 to 45 lbs.

Long ribs, light, about 18 to 20 lbs; heavy, 20 to 25 lbs.

Long cut hams, light, run from 12 to 14 lbs.

Long cut hams, medium, run from 16 to 18 lbs.

Long cut hams, heavy, run from 18 to 20 lbs.

Strafford hams, about 16 to 18 lbs.

Preston hams. about 16 to 18 lbs., the left bone left on.

California hams, about 10 to 12 lbs.

Picnic hams, about 8 to 10 lbs.

Boston shoulder, about 6 to 8 lbs.

When packing hams in tierces with salt, use

    21 lbs. Salt
    12 ozs. Saltpeter
    4 lbs. Granulated Sugar.

Fill up the tierce with water; roll it the same as in the sweet pickle process.

I would recommend using no pump in curing hams; my reason is that it does not make choice hams. One of the large Chicago houses has lost, in one season, over $30,000 by getting air into the hams, and now very few large packers use the pump. When you get a good, careful man to use this pump, you might take the risk, if you are in a hurry, as it cures the meat in 65 days. But it does not make choice hams.

RECIPE NO. 57

SWEET PICKLE BELLIES

The formula is the following:

¾ lb. Saltpeter
4 lbs. Granulated Sugar
75 lbs. Proof Pickle.

They take 40 days to cure.

Roll them the same as you do hams.

They should be made from nice, smooth hogs, well cut and trimmed, and to weigh within 2 lbs. each way of the average sold. When packed from the block in tierces, 300 lbs. of green meat to be packed in the same tierce, pickled according to the standard used by the packer, who brands his name upon each package.

RECIPE NO. 58

HOW MEAT SHOULD BE TREATED BEFORE YOU START PACKING IT

Hogs, from the time they are killed, should hang 48 hours before cutting up in a temperature of 35 to 36 degrees Fahrenheit, or colder.

After cutting, hams and shoulders should be spread out on racks for 48 hours before packing, in the same temperature (35 to 36 degrees Fahrenheit, or lower). This will get all the animal heat out of them, and is the great secret in curing meats. Be sure that all the animal heat is out, *then go ahead.*

RECIPE NO. 59

FOR CURING BACK PORK

Take from 35 to 40 pieces; use 10 lbs. rock salt, coarse; 8 ozs. saltpeter.

Fill barrels with 90 degrees proof pickle. This will cure clear pork or back pork; this sells for either family pork or back pork, and can be branded as such.

Cut this square and uniform.

A short rib about 35 to 40 average makes back and belly. Put the back into backs or family pork, and the bellies go for sweet pickled bellies.

Shoulders should be cut off with two ribs left on the square.

RECIPE NO. 60

RIB BELLIES

Should be cut regular and uniform in width, square at ends, edges smoothly trimmed, but not strapped. The meat should be fully cured when packed and the pieces classified in packing, extreme weights not to be used in making any specified average. Boxes to be made as near as practicable to fit the different sizes.

This meat is packed in boxes from 500 to 600 lbs., in dry salt.

RECIPE NO 61

CLEAR BELLIES

Should be cut the same as Rib Bellies, with the exception that all the bone is taken out This meat is packed in boxes from 500 to 600 lbs., in dry salt.

On an 8 or 10-lb. average belly, leave the rib in.

On clear belly, 10 or 12 lbs., take the rib out.

You can make these 12 to 14 lbs., according to your trade. Heavy bellies can be sold 12 to 14 lbs. average, and light ones from 10 to 12 lbs. average. Light bellies are always worth more than heavy ones.

In making a choice belly, always be sure to cut the seed out. What is meant by seed is this: A sow pig, after she loses her young, dries up, and the milk goes into what is called the seed. This is very objectionable when making a sale, and will not pass inspection.

RECIPE NO. 62

WHAT CONSTITUTES PRIME MESS PORK

This is cut from the whole side, except ham, which is taken off first. Then split the side right through the middle. Chop shank and foot off.

Now take the back and cut it into four pieces up to the blade. Make two pieces out of the balance.

Then chop flank square; make 4-lb. pieces up to the shank; if the other is over 6 lbs., cut it in two parts. Otherwise let it go as one.

A barrel of prime mess pork contains

20 pieces Coarse
30 pieces Prime.

The prime is made up to the blade, and the bellies up to the shank. The prime pieces must weigh 115 lbs., and the coarse, 75 lbs. When taken out the whole will weigh 310 lbs., 40 days old.

In packing, use a little fine salt between each layer, and 6 ozs. saltpeter, with 10 lbs. coarse salt, and fill the barrel up with 90 degrees proof pickle.

In following up this process you can rely upon getting a fine color and choice goods. In making prime mess pork take about 40 average, or between 35 and 40. Leave the shoulder on and split through the middle.

Barrels should not be required to be iron hooped unless so stipulated at time of sale.

RECIPE NO. 63

MESS PORK

In making mess pork, the ham and shoulder should be cut from the side of well fatted hogs in strips, the hog to be first split through the backbone, or, if split on one side, then an equal proportion of hard and soft sides must be packed; in cutting the shoulder off, cut the butt narrow, then cut pieces from 5 ½ to 6 ½ inches wide. On the flank, cut square pieces.

In packing mess pork, say twelve pieces to the barrel, it will take three sides. Pack two shoulders in the bottom of the barrel; one flank, then one shoulder; two middles; and always save three good pieces for header.

Pack the balance in the third row.

Use 20 lbs. fine salt; 20 lbs. coarse salt.

Put one-third coarse in the bottom of the barrel; mix fine salt between the pork and put two-thirds coarse salt on top. Fill the barrel with water, or you may use 20 lbs. coarse salt, and fill with pickle 100 degrees proof. But I think that using salt will give best satisfaction.

Pack 290 lbs. to the barrel; this must be *ex-*

act In about six months this will weigh 306 lbs., which is regular. If older, it will weigh from 315 to 318 lbs.

Break this down twice. First, after 10 days; second, after 20 days.

If cutting heavy pieces, 10 pieces are worth more than 12 pieces. A premium of 25 cents per barrel is aways paid for 10 pieces in preference to 12 pieces. Twelve pieces are worth more than 14 pieces. But do not go over 14 pieces to the barrel, as it will not be regular if you do.

When packed fresh from the block, 190 lbs of green meat is to be weighed in.

RECIPE NO. 64

LIGHT LONG CLEARS

Light long clears must be cut square; the backbone must be taken off and the ribs taken out, the slip-bone sawed down even with the meat.

Long cut hams are cut from long cut clears that would leave no split bone, and, consequently, would need no sawing. The blade should be taken out with a small pocket, and the shoulder bone should be taken out with the shank and side. Leaf lard should be scraped clean out of the belly, and cut square at each end. You can use the same cure as is used in curing long cut hams.

RECIPE NO. 65

NEW YORK SHOULDERS

New York shoulders should be made from small, smooth hogs.

Shank cut off one inch above the knee joint.

Butted about one inch from the blade-bone.

Neck and breast flap taken off.

Trimmed close and smooth. Reasonably uniform in size.

And to average, in lots, not to exceed fourteen pounds.

Three hundred pounds, block weight, should be packed in each tierce.

Pickle same as used for hams.

RECIPE NO. 66

SHORT FAT BACKS

Short fat backs should be made from sides of heavy, well-fatted hogs from which the bellies have been cut.

Backbone and ribs taken out.

All lean taken off. To be trimmed smoothly and properly squared on all edges.

Packed in dry salt in boxes of five hundred to six hundred lbs.

RECIPE NO. 67

SHORT RIB SIDES

To make short rib sides, the bone should be taken out.

The backbone and breast bone sawed or cut down smooth and even with the face of the side.

Feather of blade bone not to be removed, and no incision (pocket) to be made in side.

Packed in boxes of about five hundred pounds.

RECIPE NO. 68

LONG FAT BACKS.

Long fat backs should be cut regular and uniform in width, square at ends. Sparerib and blade bone taken out.

Lean to be cut out smooth and even with face of side.

Edges to be smoothly trimmed.

Meat to be fully cured when packed.

Pieces to be classified in packing.

This meat is packed in boxes to fit, from five hundred to six hundred pounds. Dry salt.

RECIPE NO. 69

SHORT CLEAR BACKS

Short clear backs should be made from the sides of smooth hogs, from which the bellies have been cut, backbone and ribs taken out, and lean left on, tail-bone sawed off even with the face of the meat and trimmed smooth and square on all the edges.

Packed in boxes to fit them, five to six hundred pounds, in dry salt.

RECIPE NO. 70

EXTRA LONG CLEARS

Extra long clear should be cut and trimmed in all respects like long clear, except that in addition all the loin should be neatly trimmed off down to the fat.

Packed in boxes to fit the meat, five hundred to six hundred pounds, in dry salt.

RECIPE NO. 71

LONG CLEARS

Long clears should be cut reasonably square at both the tail end and the shoulder end.

The neck taken off and smoothly trimmed.

Backbone, shoulder bone and ribs taken out.

Leg bone and blade, hench bone and breast bone sawed off; or cut down smooth and even with the face of the side.

Packed in boxes to fit the meat, five hundred to six hundred pounds, in dry salt.

RECIPE NO. 72

CUMBERLAND CUTS

Cumberland sides should have the end from which the ham is taken cut square.

The leg cut off below the knee joint.

The shoulder, ribs, neck bone, backbone and blood vein taken out, the breast bone saved, or cut down smooth and even with the face of the side, and should not be back strapped or flanked.

Clean out the belly and cut the end square.

These cuts must be free from seed and old sows. They must strictly come from choice hogs. The cure for them is the same as for long cut hams and clears.

They should be cured by dipping in pickle and then put in a box and rubbed lightly with salt. Put most of the salt on the back and shoulder, as these are the thickest parts to be cured.

Use 2 ounces saltpeter on each side; pile them eight high. It takes 15 to 20 days before they are ready for shipment. Overhaul them in 5 days, and again in 10 days. Do not salt this meat too heavily.

In packing this meat for shipment, put a layer of salt, about one inch thick, in the bottom; then rub the cuts through a box and sprinkle a handful of salt on shoulder and back. On the top side of box put a good layer of salt, and turn the skin side up.

Packed in boxes from 500 to 600 lbs., in dry salt.

RECIPE NO. 73

WILTSHIRE SIDES

Wiltshire sides should be made from smooth hogs.

The shoulder, side and ham must be left together in one piece.

The blade-bone must be taken out.

Foot cut off the shoulder same as a Cumberland. Hip bone taken out.

Not to be back strapped. Belly to be trimmed up even. Leg of the ham to be cut off above the joint.

Packed in boxes to fit the meat, four hundred to five hundred pounds.

RECIPE NO. 74

SOUTH STAFFORDSHIRE SIDES

South Staffordshire sides should be made the same as Birmingham, except loin taken out full to top of shoulder blade, leaving only a thin strip of lean along the back.

Knuckle left in and cut off close to the breast.

Packed in boxes to fit the meat, five hundred to six hundred pounds, in dry salt.

RECIPE NO 75

LONG RIB MIDDLES

Long rib middles should be the same as Cumberlands except, that the blade bone must be taken out, and the leg cut off close to the breast.

Should be packed in boxes to fit the meat, four to five hundred pounds per box, in dry salt or borax as may be ordered.

RECIPE NO. 76

SHORT CUT MESS PORK

Short cut mess pork is made from heavy fat hogs. Bellies stripped off, and similar to family pork, excepting that it is made from very heavy hogs. Has all the bone and lean on the meat.

RECIPE NO. 77

SHORT CLEAR MIDDLES

Short clear middles should be cut reasonably square at each end.

The backbone and ribs to be taken out.

Hench bone and breast bone sawed or cut down smooth and even with the face of the side.

Feather of blade bone not to be removed, and no incision (pocket) to be made in the side.

Packed in boxes from five hundred to six hundred pounds, in dry salt.

RECIPE NO. 78

BIRMINGHAM SIDES

They are cured the same as Cumberland and Long Clear. They are as follows:

Saw the backbone off and take ribs out, then raise the blade bone; make a saucer pocket; cut shank off at joint close to the breast; then take a thin slice of lean meat off the back and cut end square.

Packed in boxes to fit the meat, 500 to 650 pounds, and packed in dry salt.

RECIPE NO. 79

YORKSHIRE CUTS

The backbone and ribs being out, cut the shank about one inch above the first join and square the ends. Always use the thickest backs for Yorkshire cuts and use the others for Cumberlands and Birminghams.

They should be packed in boxes to fit the meat, 500 to 600 pound in dry salt.

RECIPE NO. 80

LONG RIB CUTS

Saw the backbone and take out one rib with the neck bone and the blade bone; but make a small pocket and twist the shoulder bone out with the shank.

RECIPE NO. 81

STAFFORDSHIRE HAMS

Staffordshire Hams should be cut short.

Hip bone taken out at socket joint.

Hock unjointed at first joint below the hock joint.

Cured and packed as directed.

RECIPE NO. 82

SHORT CUT CLEAR PORK.

Short cut clear pork should be cut and packed in the same manner as backs, except that three inches of the belly end may be left on each strip, with not exceeding three inches of bone on any strip.

Packed five layers to the barrel.

RECIPE NO. 83

MANCHESTER HAMS

Manchester Hams should be made in all respects like the Staffordshire Hams, except that the hip bone must be left in. Cured and packed as directed.

RECIPE NO. 84

PRESTON CUTS

Cut in the same manner as for Staffordshire ham, only leave the left bone on.

RECIPE NO. 85

CALIFORNIA HAMS

This shoulder should weigh 18 to 20 lbs. and be cut one inch from the joint; this takes the butt off; trim it round.

In this cut there is a lop of lean meat; this is over the blade.

Lift this up and cut it and the blob fat off. That makes the California ham look lean, and is just what is wanted. Cut shank off to expose the marrow about 1½ inches above first joint.

Trim as well on the face as possible. Breast flap taken off.

Make it reasonably uniform in size and average. If cured in pickle, handle the same as American short cut ham and pack as required.

RECIPE NO. 86

PICNIC HAMS

They are made according to the preceding recipe, except that lighter hogs are used.

RECIPE NO. 87

BOSTON SHOULDERS

Boston shoulder shall be cut straight to lean meat on both sides.

Blades cut not over three inches from shoulder, joint well trimmed, square on top or fat slightly trimmed under on butt end.

Neck bone and short ribs taken out.

Blood vein lifted and cut out.

Breast flap trimmed off. Foot to be cut off above knee joint.

Packed in sweet pickle, in tierces of three hundred pounds each, in boxes of five hundred to six hundred pounds, in dry salt or borax as ordered.

RECIPE NO. 88

LONG CUT HAMS

Long cut hams should be cut from the side by separating with a knife the hip bone from the rump, properly rounded out, foot unjointed at first joint below the hock joint.

Cured in dry salt. Packed in dry salt and in boxes from four hundred and fifty to six hundred and fifty pounds as required.

RECIPE NO. 89

AMERICAN SHORT CUT HAMS

American short cut hams should be cut short and well rounded at the butt, properly faced. Shank cut off enough above hock joint to expose the marrow.

To be reasonably uniform in size.

To average sixteen pounds. No ham to weigh over eighteen pounds nor less than fourteen pounds.

When packed in tierces, three hundred pounds of block weight shall be packed in each tierce, with standard sweet pickle used by the curer.

When cured they are also packed in boxes, containing five hundred to six hundred pounds, and may be packed either in dry salt or borax as desired.

If taken from pickle, a proper percentage shall be allowed for drainage, say from three to five per cent, according to the season of the year in which the hams are packed.

This ham is also cured in dry salt and sugar for some markets.

RECIPE NO. 90

SHORT CLEARS PACKED FOR EXPORT

These are made from heavy hogs, from 7 to 9 pieces and from 8 to 10 pieces per barrel.

These are cut exactly like short ribs, only the backbone is taken out and cleared. These are cured in American salt, no saltpeter being used.

The backbone, breastbone and ribs are all taken out, and the hench bone sawed smooth and even with the face of the side; feather of the blade bone not to be taken out; edges to be left smooth; sides not to be back strapped or flanked, and packed in boxes from 500 to 600 lbs. in dry salt.

RECIPE NO. 91

EXTRA SHORT CLEARS

Same as short clears, with the exception that all of the lean meat is taken off from the sides.

Packed in boxes from 500 to 600 pounds, in dry salt.

RECIPE NO. 92

EXTRA SHORT CUTS

These are made from lighter hogs, 35 to 45 average. Scribe the rib with a saw just even to the meat; this makes a line of pork. Cure this in the same manner as short clears. The great demand for these comes from the South.

RECIPE NO. 93

SHORT RIBS

Raise the backbone and saw it off; take tenderloins out, scrape leaf lard out, and cure the same as long clears.

Packers generally figure one day to the pound for cure; thus a 40-lb. piece would take about 40 days, etc.

RECIPE NO. 94

EXPORT SHORT RIB

Export short ribs should be cut similar to short rib middles, excepting that they should be nearly square at each end, and average as to sizes with uniformity. To be packed as ordered for markets intended for.

RECIPE NO. 95

THREE RIB SHOULDER

This is cut from the side, between the third and fourth rib; that leaves three ribs on the shoulder. Then raise the ribs and neck bone off, but leave all the meat on the shoulder; it must be smooth. Trim all the blood off the neck and cut even with the lean meat. Saw off the foot above the first joint, square.

Cure the same as you do long cuts.

For export have these cuts uniform, averaging 15 to 17 lbs.

They should be made from smooth, fat hogs.

Cured and packed as directed.

RECIPE NO. 96

ROLLED SHOULDER BONELESS

Rolled shoulders boneless are made by taking the bone entirely from the shoulder; rolled and tied with string and marked:

"Rolled Shoulders Boneless."

RECIPE NO. 97

ROLLED HAM BONELESS

Rolled hams boneless are made by taking the bone entirely from the ham; rolled, tied with a string and marked:

"Rolled Ham Boneless."

RECIPE NO. 98

FOOD FOR STOCK

The following table shows the number of pounds of various products, used as food for stock, which are equivalent in value to 10 pounds of hay.

Food	lbs.
Barley	5 to 6
Cabbage	20 to 30
Carrots, red	25 to 30
Carrots, white	40 to 45
Clover, green	40 to 50
Indian corn	5 to 7
Mangel-wurzel	30 to 35
Oats	4 to 7
Oil-cake	2 to 4
Peas and beans	3 to 5
Potatoes	20 to 25
Barley straw	20 to 40
Oat straw	20 to 40
Pea straw	10 to 15
Wheat straw	40 to 50

RECIPE NO. 99

TABLE OF CORN, WHAT IT WILL PRODUCE IN PORK

One bushel of corn will make 10½ lbs. of pork, gross.

With Corn at 12½ cents per bushel, Pork costs 1½ cents per lb.

With Corn at 17 cents per bushel, Pork costs 2 cents per lb.

With Corn at 25 cents per bushel, Pork costs 3 cents per lb.

With Corn at 35 cents per bushel, Pork costs 4 cents per lb.

With Corn at 42 cents per bushel, Pork costs 5 cents per lb.

With Corn at 50 cents per bushel, Pork costs 6 cents per lb.

RECIPE NO. 100

FOOD FOR SHEEP

The following table shows the number of pounds, live weight, and the number of pounds of wool and of tallow produced by 1,000 lbs. of each of the articles named, when used as food for sheep:

Kind of Food	Increase in weight, pounds	Wool produced, pounds	Tallow produced, pounds
Barley	136	11½	60
Buckwheat	120	10	33
Corn meal, wet	129	13½	17½
Mangel-wurzel, raw	38½	5¼	6½
Oats	146	10	42½
Peas	134	14½	41
Potatoes, raw, with salt	46½	6½	12½
Potatoes, raw, without salt	44	6½	11½
Rye, with salt	133	14	35
Rye, without salt	90	12	43
Wheat	155	14	69½

FACTS AND ADVICE FOR BUILDING PACKING HOUSES

One-fifth more siding and flooring is needed than the number of square feet of surface to be covered, on account of the lap in siding and matching of flooring.

A cord of stone, 3 bushels of lime and 1 cubic yard of sand will lay 100 cubic feet of wall.

Twenty two cubic feet of stone, when built into a wall, is one perch.

Three pecks lime and 4 bushels sand are required to each perch of wall.

There are 20 common bricks in a cubic foot when laid, and 15 common bricks to 1 foot of an 8-inch wall when laid.

Five courses of brick will lay 1 foot in height. On a chimney, 8 bricks in a course will make a flue 4 inches wide and 10 inches long.

One bushel cement and 2 bushels sand will cover $3\frac{1}{2}$ square yards 1 inch thick, or $4\frac{1}{2}$ square yards $\frac{3}{4}$ inch thick, or $6\frac{3}{4}$ square yards $\frac{1}{2}$ inch thick.

One bushel cement and 1 bushel sand will cover $2\frac{1}{4}$ square yards 1 inch thick, or 3 square yards ¾ inch thick, or 4½ square yards ½ inch thick.

Two thousand shingles laid 4 inches to the weather will cover 200 square feet of roof, and 10½ lbs. of 4-penny nails will fasten them on.

PILING UP TIERCES

A great many packers, when piling up tierces, will be glad to know the amount of surface feet it will take to store 1,000 tierces piled up three high. The space will be exactly 43 feet long and 64 feet wide, or 2,750 square feet.

This allows 6 feet for alley.

THE ANDERSON . . . .
Dryers, Deodorizers, Tanks, etc.

Owing to the improved methods of treating tankage, blood, etc., the time has come when no packer, butcher or fertilizer concern, can afford to be without machinery to convert the offal from their plant into a marketable product, and thus cause that which has been a waste and loss to become an article of profit, and in many instances remove what has been an annoyance to the community. To accomplish all of this, one must be equipped with the best and most economical machinery, and that which is absolutely sanitary in operation, for by observing this last feature, one can locate his plant in almost any desirable location, and keep within the sanitary restrictions of the health authorities, —and to no one is the packer, butcher or fertilizer concern more indebted than to the V. D. Anderson Company, of Cleveland, Ohio, for the present efficient machinery used in conducting this branch of their work, for by years of experience and costly experiments the Anderson Company have produced the most perfect, economical and sanitary fertilizer machinery ever put on the market, and have adapted it in capacity and cost to meet the requirements of all the varied conditions of the trade, from the largest to the smallest concern.

The Anderson Dryer is the most perfect dryer made, and embodies all of the correct principles of a tankage, blood or fertilizer dryer, is economical to operate, and is built of the best materials and in the most workman-like manner possible,—it has no equal.

The Anderson Deodorizer, the purpose of which is to destroy the offensive odors that come from rendering tanks, through the blow-off pipe, while rendering and when blowing down,—will absolutely destroy all such odors. It is simple in construction, easy to operate and not liable to get out of order. It is the only pefect Tank Deodorizer, and has made it possible to use tanks in localities where rendering has heretofore been prohibited. It can be connected to any rendering tank.

The Anderson Company manufacture tanks of every style and description, always aiming to give their patrons the latest and most improved ideas known.

See advertisement on page 1.

Fuller's Earth

The leading Importers of Fuller's Earth, so extensively used for bleaching and refining of Lard, Cottonseed and other animal and vegetable Oils, Tallow, Greases, etc., are L. A. SALOMON & BRO., 216 Pearl Street, New York. Their Fuller's Earth is considered the best in the market and is used by the principal Refiners in the United States and Canada. The author of Winter's Handy Book of Reference for Packers, Butchers, etc., having personally had frequent occasions to use their Fuller's Earth, can highly recommend it to the trade.

www.ingramcontent.com/pod-product-compliance
Lightning Source LLC
Chambersburg PA
CBHW030336170426
43202CB00010B/1149